Battleground
ZEEBRUGGE
AND OSTEND RAIDS 1918

Battleground series:

With the continued expansion of the Battleground Series a **Battleground Series Club** has been formed to benefit the reader. The purpose of the Club is to keep members informed of new titles and to offer many other reader-benefits. Membership is free and by registering an interest you can help us predict print runs and thus assist us in maintaining the quality and prices at their present levels.

Please call the office on 01226 734555, or send your name and address along with a request for more information to:

Battleground Series Club Pen & Sword Books Ltd,
47 Church Street, Barnsley, South Yorkshire S70 2AS

Battleground Europe
ZEEBRUGGE
AND OSTEND RAIDS 1918

Stephen McGreal

Pen & Sword
MILITARY

This book is dedicated to Agnes,
my hardworking and loving Mum.

First published in Great Britain in 2007 by
LEO COOPER
an imprint of
Pen & Sword Books Ltd
47 Church Street
Barnsley
South Yorkshire
S70 2AS

Copyright © Stephen McGreal 2007

ISBN 9781-84415608-5

Typeset in Times by
Phoenix Typesetting, Auldgirth, Dumfriesshire

Printed and bound in England by
CPI UK

Pen & Sword Books Ltd incorporates the imprints of Pen & Sword Aviation, Pen &
Sword Maritime, Pen & Sword Military, Wharncliffe Local History, Pen & Sword Select,
Pen & Sword Military Classics and Leo Cooper.

For a complete list of Pen & Sword titles please contact
PEN & SWORD BOOKS LIMITED
47 Church Street, Barnsley, South Yorkshire, S70 2AS, England
E-mail: enquiries@pen-and-sword.co.uk
Website: www.pen-and-sword.co.uk

CONTENTS

Built in 1953 *Royal Iris* **is the third Wallasey ferry to bear the name. Sold in 1991, she now lies a rotting hulk near the Millennium Dome in London.**

The Zeebrugge and Ostend Raids 1918

This is a new departure for the **Battleground Europe** series – a book devoted to actions almost entirely manned by members of the Royal Navy. Of course the raids themselves are worthy of such a book, but it is also useful to be reminded occasionally that the Royal Navy contributed a vital component of the fighting that resulted in success in November 1918. It worked tirelessly to keep the sea lanes opened, developed new technologies to deal with the innovations that the Germans introduced to counter British naval power and, of course, it effectively made impotent the huge fleet that Germany had built in the years prior to the war. Most of this work was tedious and uninspiring – blockading, convoy duty and remaining on high alert for a fleet breakout could hardly be anything else. This did not stop it, however, from being both dangerous and essential for the war effort.

It is at least doubtful if the Zeebrugge Raid actually achieved its key objective or really hindered the German submarines unduly. But actions are not only measured in how far they lived up to a particular objective. The submarine war was, in a sense, already won – or at least well on the way to being won – by the time that the Raids were carried out. But the news of the Raids broke at a crucial moment for the morale of the nation. Although the initial German onslaughts of 1918 had been halted before Amiens and Ypres, the last kicks of the offensives on the Somme and in Flanders were still being played out when the Zeebrugge Raid actually took place. Indeed, there was still steam left in the German 'Spring Offensive', as was shown with the major attack around Rheims in late May.

The British public needed a morale boosting action and they got it. It was also an illustration of British naval power, equally significant at this time, especially after many months when German U Boat successes had had a significant impact on civilians through the rationing system.

The Raids showed extraordinary levels of heroism and grim determination; the men who fought and often died in them deserve to be better remembered and Stephen McGreal has admirably succeeded in doing that.

NIGEL CAVE,
The Vercors, Summer 2007

AUTHOR'S INTRODUCTION

During the formative years of my childhood, my family moved from the terrace streets of Liverpool to the then semi-rural Wirral. In pre-car owner days this effectively severed our ties with our extended Liverpool family and visits to our relatives required a lengthy bus and ferry boat trip across the then bustling River Mersey. It was possibly on one such trip that I became aware of the role undertaken by two Wallasey ferries during the dark days of the First World War. My young imagination worked over-time as I tried to understand the task so bravely undertaken by such small vessels during the April 1918 raid on Zeebrugge.

In recognition of the naval exploits of *Iris* and *Daffodil*, King George V awarded both ferries a Royal prefix, hence *Royal Daffodil* and *Royal Iris*. Only three ferries now ply their trade across the river: two possess the names of their battle-scarred predecessors. Annually the Merseyside branch of the Royal Marine Association holds a memorial service and a mid-river church service aboard either the current *Royal Iris* or *Royal Daffodil*. In recent times, a stone block engraved with the Royal Navy and Royal Marine cap badges with suitable inscription, sited at Seacombe terminus, has become the focus point for the floral tributes and wreaths. Although the original Zeebrugge and Ostend participants have long passed on, several octogenarian members of the Royal Marines Association, [Merseyside] continue to commemorate their fallen comrades who fell at Zeebrugge 1918 and Walcheren 1944.

Almost nine decades later the raid's anniversary continues to be commemorated at Wallasey, Dover and Zeebrugge – such is its historical significance. It is an honour to be permitted the opportunity to write this small volume on an operation described thus.

'The raid on Zeebrugge may well rank as the finest feat of arms in the Great War, and certainly as an episode unsurpassed in the history of the Royal Navy'

Winston Churchill. 1918.

In 1998, the Seacombe memorial was unveiled. An annual ceremony is held here on the nearest Sunday to St. George's Day.

ACKNOWLEDGEMENTS

This book would not have been possible without the co-operation of many helpful people who have generously helped in my quest for information on Zeebrugge or Ostend combatants. I offer my sincere thanks to the following helpful people. To Roni Wilkinson for suggesting my knowledge of the Zeebrugge and Ostend operations would make a welcome addition to this series. To my wife Ann and grown-up daughter Nicola who made my research trip more pleasurable: some holiday acting as a secretary carefully recording headstones' details!

The Royal Marines Museum, Southsea, Hampshire, in particular their documentation archivist, Mathew Little, for kindly providing information on the 4th Battalion Royal Marines. Iain MacKenzie, Curatorial Officer, Admiralty Library, Ministry of Defence for the wealth of information he supplied on Royal Naval and RMLI Zeebrugge casualties and for copies of the Memoirs of Sergeant Harry Wright. The Commonwealth War Graves Commission for their assistance; it would be remiss of me to fail to applaud their staff for their dedicated care of the memorials and cemeteries entrusted to their care. Commissaris Freddy Vervaet for the courtesy shown to the author during a whirlwind visit minutes before the Hull ferry departed. Philip Bastow. Larry Clow. Mrs Done, Wallasey library. George Donnison. Richard Forrester. John and Marie Hulme for the image and details of marine Eddie Grayken. Ron Lankshear for the photograph and information on Eddy Lankshear. Kevin McCormack. Tom Parry. Patricia and Arthur Rowland for the photographs of Private Aldridge. Peter Threlfall. The *Wallasey News* editor Sue McCann. The *Wirral Globe* editor Leigh Marles. The Royal Marines Association [Merseyside] and Mersey Travel for continuing the traditional Wallasey service of remembrance.

An imaginative depiction of the raid which appeared in a popular magazine at the time.

SENSIBLE ADVICE FOR TRAVELLERS

Considering Zeebrugge is one of the gateways to Europe, it seems very odd that the region does not attract a wider audience of Great War buffs. Far from being the bustling container port we might expect, the sprawling coastal town is in fact a relatively quiet and relaxed area of Belgium. The region appears devoid of battlefield coach tours; during our few days' April break we failed to notice a vehicle bearing a British number plate. If you want something a little different from the more congested and more familiar Western Front sites this may be the tour for you.

Using this pocket guide, you should be able to visit the key locations in one day, but to enjoy your visit and to allow time to take in the tourist sights, two days would make a less hectic break. There are also unconnected Belgium war memorials and a section of the Atlantic wall to visit. There is little point in visiting any battle location in a hurry. In order to appreciate the significance of the specific site allow some time for reflection and appraisal at each halt. While some battlefield guides strongly recommend you kit yourself out with rucksacks, first aid kits, compasses etc, this guide contains walks for 'softies': all you require are sensible walking shoes, a camera and nice weather. The area is renowned for its fine seafood restaurants, offering freshly caught large mussels and huge prawns. The less adventurous will discover cottage pie or spaghetti Bolognese or even chips with mayonnaise listed on most menus. Worth noting is the fact that Belgium brews over two hundred separate types of beer, why not do as the natives do: order a drink at a roadside bistro and leisurely watch the world go by?

There are two separate legs of this tour, Zeebrugge and the small, old-fashioned, seaside city of Ostend, the latter being one of the most popular seaside resorts in Belgium. They are linked with a good road not unlike our dual carriageways; also, a regular tram service runs along this pleasant coast road. When driving keep within the specified speed limit as the police carry out routine speed traps usually in close proximity to each other. Most minor motoring offences are punishable by an immediate on the spot fine payable in cash, in the local currency, to the arresting officer. You must be able to produce your car documentation and driving licence. If you have the new type of licence you must also have the accompanying part two paper document with you.

Visitors from the United Kingdom should ensure their vehicle complies with European Motoring Requirements. A GB plate or sticker must be displayed on the rear of your vehicle or trailer. Headlamps should have beam adaptors [a self-adhesive film] fitted day or night; otherwise, your vehicle is considered unfit for use and could invalidate your insurance. Other legal requirements are advance hazard warning triangle, spare exterior bulbs, first aid kit and all vehicles are now expected to carry reflective vests for drivers and their passengers. Of course, we may not wish to bother with the items, however in the small print of most motor insurance policies, is a clause. It is the driver's responsibility to ensure his vehicle complies with the law and is roadworthy for the country he visits. If the vehicle does not comply, the insurers will repudiate liability.

Your fully comprehensive motoring insurance is usually reduced to Third Party cover when driving abroad. Notify your insurers of your travel plans; and, for about ten pounds, additional temporary cover will be arranged. You should also be aware your breakdown cover is similarly affected. Finally, if travelling by car ferry to Zeebrugge make sure you know how to disable your remote control car alarm. This is usually accomplished by manually locking the vehicle. Otherwise the motion of the ship will activate your alarm; not only will this disturb passengers, it will drain your car battery. Make sure when you leave your vehicle you take an overnight bag with you, as the car deck will be locked for the duration of the voyage.

An absolute necessity for travellers is a European Health Insurance Card [EHIC]; this replaces the old E111 form and is free. The forms can be obtained from the post office: allow a minimum of four weeks for the process to be completed. The quickest method is to visit the EHIC website www.dh.gov.uk/travellers. The EHIC card gives reciprocal rights to medical and hospital treatment arising during your trip. Not all the things you expect from the NHS are included, so travel insurance is recommended as you still may be expected to contribute towards medical treatment.

The Flemish people are very friendly and respond positively to a cheery 'Good Morning', a smile and a polite enquiry. Most people have some English or can communicate in French and will usually go out of their way to help you. The exception is cyclists who, under traffic control measures, are designated privileged road users. The cyclists do become indignant when pedestrians obstruct them and indicate their displeasure by loudly ring their bells, or worse.

There is no shortage of accommodation in either Ostend or Bruges; any travel agent will be able to offer a comprehensive package. It is financially worthwhile looking on the internet and booking your room direct. The following short list may prove useful.

www.booking.com Offers a selection of thirty-six Ostend hotels.
www.a1tourism.com/belgium For accommodation in Bruges or Ostend.

Bed and Breakfast.

Hotel Prado. Leopold II – laan 22. 8400 Oostende. Tel 0032 [0] 59 80 87 35. www.hotelprado.be This is cosy, reasonably priced, clean and very friendly. Located near the beach and the city centre. Three star rating.

Hotels.

The Strand Hotel. Zeedijk 14, Zeebrugge. Tel. 93 [0] 50 544 055.

Best Western Richmond Thonnan, Blankenberge. Tel. 1-800-372-2496.

Campsite.

Camping Dallas. Baron Ruzlettelaan 191. 8370 Blankenberge. Tel. 050-418157. Fax 050- 429279. Email camp.dallas@online.be The opening period is from 1 April to 1 October. www.vitgids.com/camping

Boat trip.

The following company conducts boat trips around Zeebrugge docks. www.euroline.be Telephone 0475 20 94 52.

HOW TO USE THIS BOOK

Frankly, there is no point visiting the monuments and memorial if we have no comprehension of their role in British military history. It is suggested that you read this book at leisure and familiarise yourself with the events of April and May 1918 before setting off. Reading this pocket guide will not only provide an insight into the blocking operations but should make your visit more enjoyable. Since the end of the First World War, large swathes of the battlefields of France and Flanders have gradually disappeared beneath the plough. The port of Zeebrugge is no exception, for it has expanded considerably; the main section of the Mole where *Vindictive* discharged her storming parties has disappeared, as has the viaduct. Yet if we use the surviving Mole extension as a landmark, in conjunction with this guide, we can still relate to where the action occurred. As the Mole has been re-developed into the P & O Ferry berth, the finest way to see the surviving Mole extension is to arrive by the Hull-Zeebrugge ferry. Once ashore the town offers several related places to visit, at Ostend you will even be able to see a bow section from HMS *Vindictive*.

Your own transport is the most convenient method of visiting the memorials and cemeteries especially as the two main areas are some distance apart. The anglicised versions of Ostend and Bruges are mainly used in this work [just as the raiders did] instead of the Flemish language Oostende and Brugge. If possible, avoid the weekend Ostend city centre traffic by walking around this pleasant West Flanders resort. The Albert Promenade fringes the sandy beach and is the venue for a weekend seafood market; a very popular tourist attraction, where the traffic moves at a snail's pace. The port of Ostend has suffered since the opening of the Channel tunnel, as only one company offers a direct passenger ferry from the United Kingdom. The community is expecting the return of at least one other company. The decline in ferry traffic is also due to travellers' preference to cross via Dover to Calais then using the A16/ E40 and A18 routes linking Calais to Ostend. With its abundance of hotels and bed and breakfasts, Ostend is also convenient for Ypres, a leisurely seventy-minute drive away. You will pass through countryside where the Belgian army established itself on the River Yser from Dixmude to the coast north of Nieuport and made their last line of defence. This battlefield area alone is worthy of a visit, as this was the fiercely contested northern tip of the front line which extended some six hundred miles to the Swiss border.

Chapter One

OUR DESIGNATED TOUR AREAS

The medieval city of Bruges is a very popular destination for coach parties attracted by its architectural beauty, horse drawn carriages and canal network. During the Middle Ages the 'Venice of the North' was connected to the Flanders coast by a wide and deep estuary called the Zwin. Traders from throughout the world sailed up the channels: as a centre for trade Bruges prospered until the beginning of the fifteenth century. The Zwin channels began to silt up and by 1421, when the channels became no longer navigable, the maritime trade abandoned Bruges for the neighbouring port of Antwerp.

In the late nineteenth century the king of Belgium, Leopold II, approved a project to restore Bruges' prosperity by constructing a canal from Bruges to the North Sea. Apart from the economic benefits, the new port would offer the Belgian military a freely accessible port unlike Antwerp, for the Dutch held the opposite bank of the River Scheldt. After prolonged discussions, in 1895 the construction began. The canal was to have a depth of twenty-four feet, leading to an outer harbour at Zeebrugge protected by an arcing sea wall suitable for vessels drawing twenty-four feet to berth alongside. This vast quay wall had no equal in Great Britain or the United States and became known as 'The Mole', derived from the classical Latin term for a massive structure. The total length of the Mole from shore to lighthouse was approximately one and a half miles. This

A view of the vast Mole breakwater.

Day trippers on the Mole. The parapet on the left increased in height as the mole extended seaward.

outer harbour not only provided a safe and easy entrance to the canal, it was the preferred option for the new generation of fast mail steamers that required quick and easy access.

The Mole consisted of four sections. The first nearest the shore was a 300 yards long stone pier, having a footpath, a road and a double railway

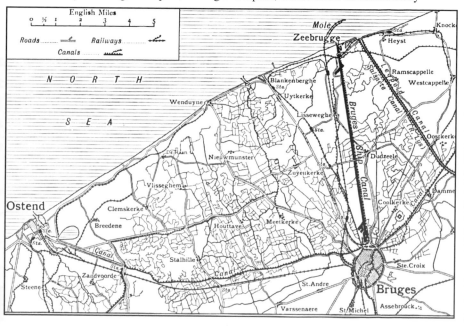

track. The next section was 300 yards long, a steel framed viaduct similar to our traditional seaside piers. The purpose of this section was to allow the tidal current to scour the internal harbour of silt. The third section, the Mole proper, was a vast construction of concrete blocks paved with granite, this was over a mile long and eighty yards wide. A huge concrete wall twenty feet high and over twelve feet thick protected the seaward side. Along this wall, four feet from its summit and sixteen feet above the main platform of the Mole, ran a seven or eight feet wide footpath, with a four-foot parapet on its seaward side and a stout iron railing on its inner side. At intervals, iron ladders or steps to the main roadway connected this walkway. At low tide the parapet was forty-four feet above sea level, even at high tide it towered thirty feet above sea level. The most distant section, the Mole extension, was a narrow pier carrying a fifteen-foot walkway: its structure conformed to that of the Mole. At the seaward tip stood a lighthouse. This final section has survived to the present day.

There was also a shallow canal from Bruges to Ostend with a branch leading to Dunkirk. Another canal existed between Bruges and Ghent; the small shallow canals could only take barges or similar shallow craft. These internal waterways could allow a small vessel to sail from Bruges to the port of Antwerp.

The port opened to trade in 1905, and steadily attracted new business. In 1913, eight hundred and eighty-eight vessels used the port, the following year the outbreak of hostilities curtailed the port's growth.

When the Germans invaded Belgium they were faced with a protective ring of forty-eight obsolete forts and small redoubts to which the Belgian

A view of the dock gate of the Zeebrugge/Bruges canal; all attempts to destroy this during the Great War failed.

Above and right: **A Royal Marine flying column marching through Ostend.**

army retired. On 28 September, the German onslaught upon Antwerp began. After repelling four days of infantry assaults and siege gun bombardments, the valiant Belgian garrison decided to withdraw. Winston Churchill, the First Lord of the Admiralty, visited Antwerp, where he implored the Belgians to hold out a little longer. British and French reinforcements were promised. The Royal Marines and naval reservists of the Royal Naval Division were despatched as a 'Flying Column' and they landed at Ostend on 4 October. No sooner had they dug in at Antwerp than the Germans established a major bridgehead; Antwerp was evacuated. Rawlinson's Regular 7th Division and the 3rd Cavalry

Division, In a fleet of twenty-two ships, disembarked at Zeebrugge between 6 and 8 October. On the first day of the landing, Commodore Roger Keyes briefly disembarked from *Lurcher* onto the Mole. He was not to know that within a few years' time his name would be forever linked with this edifice. Rawlinson's reinforcements arrived too late but did concentrate at Ghent where they covered the Belgian and Royal Naval Division withdrawal.

By mid October, the German advance swept through Belgium, successively overrunning Zeebrugge and Ostend. It is incomprehensible that the modern port of Zeebrugge was not destroyed prior to its German occupation. As the military considered the war would be over by Christmas, the retiring armies assumed the port would soon be back in Belgian possession. This was a calamitous error, for the enemy were to remain in possession until 17 October 1918; before departing they destroyed the port. The victorious Germans occupied the entire Belgian coast as far as the Yser. They now possessed an invaluable outpost some three hundred miles nearer to Dover than their naval ports in the Heligoland Bight. The reduction of mileage not only conserved fuel, it lessened the risk of interception by the Royal Navy. The German Navy was now in a strategic position from where it could threaten the British lines of communication with the Continent and her Atlantic sea traffic.

Germany lost no time in developing her acquisitions and by the end of November Zeebrugge was an operational naval base. The Bruges-Zeebrugge-Ostend canal network forms a triangle with two sea entrances. The eastern leg is an eight-mile canal from Zeebrugge to Bruges. On the southern side, the smaller canal from Ostend to Bruges covers eleven miles. The base of the triangle was the heavily defended coastal frontage

A fifteen-inch [380mm] gun of the *Deutschland* Battery, south-west of Ostend. Compare the size of the men below the barrel for an appreciation of the size of the weapon.

between Ostend and Zeebrugge.

This twelve mile long, north-west facing coastal stretch contains the sites and memorials featured in this work.

The three miles or so of sand duned coastline between Blankenburghe and Zeebrugge housed four artillery batteries. The *Zeppelin* Battery existed closest to the Mole and comprised four guns of four-inch (10cm) calibre. West of this stood the *Groden Battery* of four eleven inch howitzers, their firepower overlapped the four gun *Mittel B* defences of four-inch calibre ordnance. These were mounted on concrete bases on the crest of the sand hills and were capable of an anti-aircraft role. To the east of Blankenburghe, a set of four single barrelled six-inch weaponry stood sentinel. The four barrels of the three point five guns of the *Hafen* Battery guarded the western approaches to Blankenburghe supported by the four eight inch artillery pieces of the *Herta* Battery.

The firepower defences for Zeebrugge harbour were formidable. The sea walls bristled with a battery of four three point five inch guns and assorted three, four, six and eleven point five inch firepower. Directly in line with the tip of the Mole stood the menacing *Friedriechsart* Battery whose six point five naval guns in enclosed turrets dominated the harbour. Beyond the canal, the *Kanal B* Battery consisting of thirty-one two-inch weapons abutted a ring of steel surrounding the Belgian coast-line.

The Bruges-Zeebrugge-Ostend canal network forms a triangle with two sea entrances. The eastern leg is an eight-mile canal from Zeebrugge.

18

Chapter Two

THE PIRATES' LAIR

The Germans intensively fortified the coast from their right flank near Nieuport to the Dutch border. Eventually 225 artillery pieces were in place, the calibre of 136 of these varied from six to fifteen inch; the latter was capable of firing a shell for twenty-one miles. Near Ostend, the German *Jakobynessen* battery had fifteen-inch guns; they fired projectiles measuring over six feet long and weighing seventeen hundredweight. Their range was 60,000 yards: equivalent to thirty-four land miles. Of the two ports, Zeebrugge was the most significant, for its canal allowed the passage of destroyers and submarines from their base at Bruges. The enemy constructed seaplane sheds, bombproof submarine shelters, stores and ammunition sheds. The vessels for the Flanders Flotilla were initially small destroyers and A class submarines fabricated in Germany prior to assembly in the occupied Antwerp shipyards. The *Untersee* boats [U-boats] then passed safely through the inland canals to the Bruges naval base. Eventually, after evading the Royal Naval blockade, vessels displacing one thousand tons with a thirty-five knot speed armed with three 4.1-inch guns arrived. Ostend, despite having a

German gunners guarding the Mole. Taken by a German photographer after the raid.

A German propaganda postcard entitled 'The German battle against the English fleet off Oostende'.

wide array of quays, played a lesser role as it was regularly pounded by the fifteen-inch guns of the Royal Marine Artillery. Despite this, it offered a bolthole for enemy vessels evading the Royal Navy's Dover Patrol. Three miles west of Zeebrugge, the shallow fishing harbour at Blankenberge provided a base for thirty motor torpedo boats.

The Allies were incapable of wresting back the Flemish ports, for the demands of men and machinery were prioritised for other theatres. In 1915, the demands of Gallipoli, Mesopotamia and Egypt and the Western Front prevented any attempts to reclaim the Belgian ports. The next year the onslaught on Verdun and the Allied Somme offensive pinned down the armies' might. The 1916 failure by the Royal Navy to destroy the German High Seas fleet at the Battle of Jutland was a major opportunity lost to shorten the war. After the stalemate the German High Seas fleet retired to port, and the British Grand Fleet never had a second chance to eliminate in a stroke Germany's sea power. During the Jutland battle British armour piercing shells had broken up on contact with German armour plate; reliable new shells had to be developed. There were also delays in the introduction of depth charges and an efficient, more reliable mine. The Royal Navy could not risk an offensive in any area until their weaponry improved. The Russian Revolution in March 1917 led to the virtual collapse of the Eastern Front campaign. This allowed the deployment of German and some Austrian troops from the Eastern to the

Western Front. The deployment of these reinforcements in the spring of 1918 almost led to an Allied defeat. Scores of books detail this Allied crisis when defeat seemed almost inevitable. The reader of this book should bear in mind the unfolding events occurring elsewhere when this desperate operation happened.

The German fighting at Verdun and the Somme had cost the invader dearly in human life; they now looked elsewhere for victory. The German high command knew that without access to world trade, the British Isles would be starved of vital war supplies and foodstuffs and unable to continue the fight. A few weeks after the outbreak of war, Admiral von Pohl, the Chief of Naval Staff, proposed a submarine blockade of the British Isles. His suggestion first met with resistance for it was contrary to all the rules of the sea and risked sinking neutral shipping.

The early submarines first surfaced before ordering the merchant ship captain to surrender prior to the sinking or capture of his vessel. It was inevitable that a neutral ship would be sunk, for on 31 January the Admiralty advised British shipping companies that the flying of a neutral flag was a recognised *ruse de guerre* and not contrary to 'international law' on the proviso no act of aggression was carried out under cover of the flag. The German admirals won their argument and an announcement warned from 18 February, the waters around Britain and Ireland, including the Channel, were a War Zone and that every merchant ship in

A contemporary general view of Ostend from the station.

The US tanker Illinois. The oil tanker sailed from Port Arthur, Texas on 17 February 1917, bound for England. On 18 March, while returning to the States with a ballast cargo (seawater in tanks for stability) she was torpedoed by *UC 21*. The vessel sank twenty miles north of Alderney and eighteen miles north-west of Cherbourg. For propaganda purposes, the German U-boat crew photographed the sinking.

this zone would be destroyed. Great Britain was to be brought to her knees by the submarine war and the effective intervention of the United States was to be made impossible.

Old-world courtesy gave way to unrestricted warfare, and an outraged world dipicted this as the epitome of German barbarity. Despite the statement, high seas' chivalry still survived for, in 1915, only one-fifth of vessels went to the bottom without warning. Once the U-boats left port they were almost impossible to locate, for sonar and radar did not exist. Technology would gradually catch up with the submarine menace; by the latter stages of the war hydrophone listening equipment existed. In the meantime, decoy merchantmen plied the shipping routes hoping to gain the attention of a U-boat. Once the submarine had surfaced and ordered the abandonment of the vessel that had been or was about to be torpedoed, a well-rehearsed act of abandoning ship was performed. As this ruse was being enacted, the Q or Mystery ship skeleton crew removed the screening around their concealed gun batteries then attempted to sink the U-boat.[1] The German answer was to put the safety of the U-boat first and sank ships on sight. Several Q ships were lost with all hands in 1917, the following year their use ended. Unrestricted warfare carried a grave risk, namely the sinking of a neutral vessel, ie one from a non-belligerent country. The Atlantic sinking of the Liverpool bound Cunard passenger liner *Lusitania* by *U20* on 7 May 1915 claimed the lives of almost 1200 souls. Excluding her 700 crew, almost 800 passengers including, over one hundred Americans, drowned. Their deaths provided the American pro-war lobby with one more reason to become involved in the war, but in 1915 its participation was a long way off.

The SS *Brussels* was a Great Eastern Railway steamer that despite the war maintained a regular service on the Rotterdam to Harwich route. The enemy were determined to sink the steamer. On 3 March 1915, her captain, Charles Fryatt, sighted an enemy U-boat and the submarine set a course for the SS *Brussels*. Fryatt ordered all spare hands to the engine room to stoke the boilers, and outran the U-boat. When the ship returned to port, it returned to a hero's reception. The vessel's grateful owners presented him with a suitably engraved gold watch, recording the skill and determination of Fryatt. On 28 March 1915, Captain Fryatt again encountered a submarine, reputed to be one of the latest classes. The U-boat was 300 feet long, with a high bow and a large conning tower. Captain Fryatt knew he could not outrun this vessel. When the submarine signalled him to halt, Captain Fryatt decided to make a fight of it. He telegraphed the engine room for full speed, starboarded his helm and steered straight for the U-boat conning tower; she immediately crash-dived. Although he did not feel his ship strike the submarine, when it

No 15.

Le S.S. Brussels renfloué et son héroïque capitaine Fryatt.
The S.S. "Brussels" set afloat again and her heroic Captain Fryatt
Het stoomschip Brussels vlot gebracht. Zijn heldhaftigen kapitein Fryatt

Captain Fryatt and the re-floated SS _Brussels_.

**The Fryatt
Memorial in Bruges.**

surfaced it had a pronounced list. Once more he made his escape.

The Admiralty presented Fryatt with a watch inscribed 'Presented by the Lords Commissioners of the Admiralty to Charles Algernon Fryatt, Master of the SS _Brussels,_ in recognition of the example set by that vessel when attacked by a German submarine, 28 March 1915'. The award was also announced in the House of Commons; the British media also championed him. Unknowingly they as good as signed his death warrant.

On 22 June 1916, Captain Fryatt sailed the _Brussels_ from the Hook of Holland outward bound for Tilbury. En route, the vessel was captured by a flotilla of enemy torpedo boats and then interned in Zeebrugge. When his captives discovered the inscribed watch they accused Fryatt of being a _franc-tireur_; he was court-martialled then sentenced to death on the following grounds: 'Although he was not a member of a combatant force he made an attempt on the afternoon of 28 March 1915, to ram the German submarine _U33_ near the Maas Lightship.' By all accounts, they condemned him before the trial took place; he was buried in a small Bruges cemetery. After the war, his mortal remains were repatriated. His captured vessel became accommodation for the Zeebrugge flying boatcrews.

24

The crime caused a great outcry in Britain, where it was cited as the latest example of Hun barbarity. It was in fact a German response to a directive issued by Winston Churchill to 'immediately engage the enemy, either with their armament if they possess it, or ramming if they do not'. Churchill's orders fell into enemy hands in February 1915 when a British freighter was boarded. All Allied sea Captains were now left in no doubt of their fate should they be captured after an attempt to engage a U-boat. It was, of course, a futile attempt to bottle up Britain's merchant fleet in their harbours.

The Germans became bolder; on the night of 26 October 1916, ten destroyers of the Flanders flotilla made their first raid into the English Channel; they sank three ships, the empty transport *Queen*, the destroyer *Nubian*, and disabled the destroyer *Flirt*.

Since 1916, the Admiralty had debated the merits of attacking Zeebrugge; however, there was extreme reluctance to destroy a port they might yet recapture. Admiral Bayley in November 1916 suggested a combined naval and military operation, but the proposal fell on deaf ears. Similarly, Commodore Tywhitt, suggested the use of block ships supported by a bombardment of smoke screens and poison gas to neutralise Zeebrugge. Although this proposal was discussed at length, no action was taken, mainly due to the risks of gassing Belgian civilians. Tywhitt suggested a further scheme at the beginning of January, but this was also rejected. The plans were consigned to an Admiralty safe where they remained until February 1919.

By the beginning of 1917, one ship in every four sailing in British waters went to the bottom of the sea. In February 1917 the U-boat fleet numbered 111 vessels, the following month the sea wolves sank 900,000 tons of Allied shipping. With only six weeks' food supply left in Britain, Admiral Jellicoe on 27 April grudgingly allowed an experimental convoy to sail. The enemy submarines suddenly found themselves searching deserted seas in their quest for a

A torpedo strikes its goal.

A Flanders Flotilla U-boat leaving the Bruges canal.

victim. From September 1917, the monthly average sink tonnage was reduced to 400,000 tons.

A post-war official German report stated–

The Flanders U-boat flotilla sank 2,554 allied ships, having an aggregate tonnage of 4,400,000, or 33% of the total tonnage sunk. The losses sustained at Bruges were 80 U-boats, 145 officers and more than 1,000 men.

Commodore Tywhitt remained undeterred by past rejections and on 7 May 1917 he proposed the capture of Zeebrugge by a joint naval and military attack, as a prelude to using the port for a military advance on

UB10 moored at Zeebrugge.

Antwerp and the turning of the German flank. This time the authorities considered the scheme at great length.

Late in the summer of 1917, Sir Eric Geddes became First Lord of the Admiralty; he quickly realised the Admiralty Board needed more dynamic members. He selected Admiral Sir Rosslyn Wemyss to assist him in a more vigorous prosecution of the sea war. On arriving at the Admiralty, Wemyss was dismayed to discover the defensive nature of the Admiralty Board. It was policy to allow the enemy to take the initiative; this was in direct contrast to the offensive nature of Wemyss. Several days later, with the permission of Admiral Beatty, Wemyss visited the Grand Fleet at Rosyth, where he invited Roger Keyes to join him in the newly created post of Director of Plans. By the end of September, Keyes had established himself at the Admiralty where his new Plans Division was split in two. One half was responsible for forming plans for operations, while the other calculated the material required and its source.

Roger John Brownlow Keyes was born on October 4 1872 at Tundiani Fort, India. His father was a brigadier general in command of the Punjab Frontier. Despite his strong military ties, as soon as Keyes could voice an opinion he declared, 'he wanted to be an admiral'.

Maintenance of the Zeebrugge anti-submarine net.

Despite his very poor academic results and a crooked forearm, a result of a misaligned fracture repair to his arm, Keyes became a navy cadet. His career choice would eventually prove to be the making of him. For, while he learnt his profession, the slightly built youngster became as hard as nails. He lived a 'Boys Own' lifestyle ever on the look out for action and adventure, whenever there was a fight Keyes was in the thick of it. He became a proficient sportsman, jockey and an excellent polo player; during his participation in the latter sport he became acquainted with many influential friends. After service in South African and British waters, Keyes now commanded the appropriately named *Fame*, a destroyer stationed near Hong Kong. During the 1900 China War *Fame*, on 31 May, arrived off the coast of Taku, a defended port ninety miles from Peking. On the opposite banks of the Pei-ho river lay three modern forts, armed with seventy guns, whilst upstream, moored to the dockside, lay four fast Chinese destroyers, recently arrived from their German builder. By 3 June, the entire British China squadron and over thirty warships of assorted nationalities lay off Taku.

As the situation deteriorated, an international force decided to capture the Taku forts, even though war had yet to be declared. The Chinese response to an ultimatum to surrender the forts was to open fire on the warships. Keyes then orchestrated his pre-formulated plan to capture the Chinese destroyers with *Fame* and *Whiting*. The surprised Chinese were overwhelmed by the four boarding parties. Not a British casualty was suffered, though several Chinese were killed. When Keyes returned to the flagship to report, *Fame* received an ovation from the fleet. Three of Keyes' prize vessels were presented by the British Government to Russia, Germany and France, the fourth, HMS *Taku,* was absorbed into the Royal Navy. Although still a junior officer, he had recognised the military advantage of initiative and bold decisive action. His daring exploits would ensure the admirals would become very familiar with the name of Roger Keyes.

The forts' capture allowed shallow draft vessels to venture upstream towards Tientsin. A riverside fort at Hsi-cheng prevented passage upstream; if Tientsin was to be relieved the fort must fall. Keyes' proposals to seize the fort were firmly brushed aside as 'the impetuosity of youth'. However, in late June, Russian troops and the Naval Brigade reached Tientsin; free passage upstream was essential to support them with supplies and munitions.

Keyes pressed for the capture of Hsi-cheng; the Russians and Germans had seven gun ships and 4,000 men yet considered the operation too dangerous. Keyes was straining at the leash; after managing to secure permission for a reconnaissance of the river, he discovered the fort almost empty. In true 'who dares wins' style he dashed ashore, followed by thirty-two men. Without firing a shot they captured the fort, destroyed the six guns, then retired. Keyes remained behind to light the fuse to blow the fort arsenal. Twenty miles away the British admiral's windows rattled with the explosion and, seeing a column of smoke hundreds of feet high, he remarked 'I'll bet that's Master Roger Keyes. I only hope he isn't on top of it.' Keyes' resourcefulness had accomplished a task considered unobtainable by 4,000 men.

After the relief of Tientsin, *Fame* supplied a ferry service from the fleet to Taku; one of the passengers, General Gaslee, had served under his father and remembered Keyes as a child. He promised Keyes he would seek permission for Keyes to be his ADC and take him to Peking. The walled city was to be attacked by Japanese, Russian, American and British columns. It comes as no surprise that Keyes was at the forefront of the British attack. Only a few shots were fired as the leading troops advanced on one of the many gateways.

After scaling a thirty-foot wall with a Union flag clamped between his teeth, Keyes flew the flag so the artillery knew the British were in possession. The gate was thrown open and Keyes headed the rush towards the sluice gate entrance to the Legation Quarter. Due to Keyes' slight build, he was the only one able to squeeze through the bars. His arrival in the Legation compound heralded the ending of the siege. By nightfall, Peking had been relieved.

Keyes then went on to command the Devonport destroyer flotilla. Many senior officers were sceptical about the sea worthiness of destroyers in poor weather. During three exercises in severe gales, Keyes proved how a well-commanded group of destroyers could annihilate a battle squadron. A glowing report from an admiral led to Keyes' promotion to captain.

Vice Admiral Roger Keyes. In 1930, he was made Admiral of the Fleet. In the Second World War he worked with commando training and guided the US army in amphibious landings. He died in 1942 and is interred with his men in Dover cemetery.

After three years' service as a naval attaché, Keyes was employed in the Navy Intelligence Department, London. At the end of 1904 he was appointed naval attache at Rome, Vienna, Constantinople and Athens. In January 1908 he was appointed to command *Venus*, a second-class cruiser. After the naval manoeuvres of 1910, where Keyes again performed admirably, the rising star was offered the appointment of Inspecting Captain of Submarines. The service required a bold, young captain, a forceful character with modern ideas and an offensive spirit; Keyes ably fitted the bill. The nine-year-old submarine service considered the new weapon a purely defensive one; however, during manoeuvres the worth of the submarine was ably demonstrated. New and larger vessels were now under construction; as Keyes knew little about submarines he quickly surrounded himself with experts who did.

At the outbreak of the Great War Keyes was the senior officer at Harwich, however Commodore Tywhitt commanded the 3rd and 4th Destroyer Flotillas. Large numbers of German destroyers patrolled the Heligoland approaches and Keyes arranged an attack on this concentration of shipping. On 28 August, a combined fleet sank three enemy cruisers and a destroyer; three more destroyers were badly battered.

The Government decided to force the Dardanelles; on 8 February 1915, Keyes was notified he was to be Chief of Staff to Rear Admiral Carden who, due to ill health, was superseded by Admiral de Roebeck. The Navy's attempt to force the narrows at Gallipoli met with disaster in an uncharted minefield, where five ships were lost within a few hours. Given his losses, de Roebeck was reluctant to imperil any further vessels. Keyes urged his superiors to renew the naval attack but they decided to launch the ill-fated amphibions operation against Gallipoli. The Allies were not aware that their attempt to force the narrows had almost succeeded, for Turkish mines and armour piercing ammunition were in short supply. Had Keyes' [and Churchill's] urging to press home the naval attack been adopted, the war might have ended two years earlier. Keyes unsuccessfully pressed for this action throughout the bitter campaign. He described the Gallipoli evacuation as, 'one of the most disastrous and cowardly surrenders in the history of our country'.

Due to the loss of life at the Battle of Jutland promotions became available; Keyes was summoned to London where he learnt of his imminent promotion to rear admiral. In the meantime, he was to command the cruiser *Centurion,* based at Scapa Flow. Late in November 1916, Sir John Jellicoe was appointed First Sea Lord. Admiral Beatty succeeded him; at the same time de Roebeck was appointed to command the second battle squadron, which again threw Keyes and de Roebeck together. By January 1917, false rumours circulated that as soon as Keyes received promotion he would go to Dover to replace Admiral Bacon in command of the Dover Patrol.

Keyes was promoted rear admiral on 10 April 1917; he was now forty-four. In 1917 his son Geoffrey was born; he would die in 1941 when he gained the Victoria Cross.[2] A couple of months later, a rear admiral's appointment became available. Keyes briefly joined *Colossus,* as second in command of the 4th Battle Squadron, before taking up the newly created position of Director of Plans within the Admiralty. Before he departed, the officers and warrant officers of *Centurion* presented him with a teak casket containing a huge rear admiral's silk ensign.

The success of the U-boats raised concerns within the Admiralty; an urgent solution was required to counter the menace. All attempts to mine the waters around German bases in the Heligoland Bight were ineffective for German minesweepers soon swept them clear. An alternative was to destroy the U-boats as they passed around the tip of Scotland or through the English Channel. The shorter route through the Straits of Dover reduced the U-boat journey to the Atlantic by eight days but, according to the Admiralty, an effective net barrage blocked their passage. Admiral Sir Reginald Bacon had designed the net barrages and considered them almost ninety per cent effective, a view endorsed by the Admiralty.

At the end of September the Director of Naval Intelligence informed the recently appointed Keyes that, contrary to popular belief, a steady stream of submarines passed through the Dover straits. Several days later captured German documentation revealed thirty submarines a month were using this route. While laying mines off the Waterford coast *UC44*

U-boat berthed at the Mole.

fell victim to a mine. After her salvage, papers found onboard revealed the method for avoiding the Dover net barrage.

It is best to pass this on the surface. If forced to dive, go down to forty metres.... As far as possible pass through the area Hoofden-Cherbourg without being observed or stopping. On the other hand, the boats, which in exceptional cases pass round Scotland, are to let themselves be seen as freely as possible in order to mislead the English.

By this simple sleight of hand, the enemy had duped the Admiralty Board into believing they had an almost impenetrable defence requiring no further improvement. Admiral Bacon, now convinced of the flaw in his defence, decided to establish a new minefield across the southern part of the straits. After presiding over an Admiralty committee investigating the failure of the existing net barrage, Keyes suggested a scheme for the immediate improvement of the channel defences. He insisted some provision be made to prevent the U-boats sailing on the surface under the cover

Intense activity within the 'Kapersnest' Pirates' Lair, Zeebrugge.

Photograph taken on 23 October 1918 at the shore end of the Mole. In the foreground is a 150mm gun of the Lubeck battery.

of darkness. Destroyers equipped with substantial searchlights and trawlers using flares to illuminate the minefield should patrol the barriers.

Commodore Tywhitt's earlier suggestion continued to be debated for almost six months and by 3 December 1917 the Admiralty had formulated the framework for an operation against Zeebrugge. When asked for his views, Vice-Admiral Bacon, who had commanded the Dover Patrol since April 1915, replied

> In his opinion a military operation of this nature was impracticable. Yet if treated as a raid, with the sole purpose of destroying the lock at Zeebrugge, the plan might be worth consideration. The odds on a raiding party or even a block ship being able to reach the canal were microscopic, and he urged the use of a twelve-inch naval gun to destroy the lock gates.'

As 200 heavy coastal guns protected the approaches to the ports, Keyes at first agreed no block ship could hope to reach its intended destination unaided.

During a naval battle, an outgunned or damaged warship might emit thick acrid smoke in sufficient quantity to mask her retreat from the engagement. The smoke apparatus produced a bright flame, ruling out its use in night operations. If an improved method for laying smokescreens could be developed, a block ship under cover of darkness enshrouded in

One of the coastal guns protecting the harbour. The viaduct and Mole can be seen in the background.

an artificial fog could approach a harbour unseen.

Keyes' department set about amending the proposed scheme to an outline of an attack launched simultaneously on both ports. Three old cruisers escorted by a fleet of destroyers and small coastal craft under an improved protective smokescreen would attack Zeebrugge. Three cruisers [later reduced to two] would be scuttled between the piers at Ostend. The memorandum resolved all the objections raised by the First Sea Lord and by Admiral Bacon.

> *At first sight, the blocking operation may be regarded, particularly at Zeebrugge as a hazardous enterprise. But I feel very strongly that we shall not be asking the personnel engaged to take any greater risk than the infantry and tank personnel are subjected to on every occasion on which an attack is delivered on shore.*

> Keyes

Keyes forwarded the plan to the First Sea Lord on 3 December; it was intended to be delivered to Admiral Wemyss who, had approved the plan, who would in turn forward it to the First Sea Lord. Due to a mix-up within the Admiralty office, the plan arrived on the desk of Admiral Bacon, with a request for a committee of Dover Patrol officers to examine and report on the plan. Three days later Keyes heard of the error, he took another copy to Wemyss, and explained the fate of the original memorandum.

Wemyss was furious when he heard it had been submitted to a committee as the Admiralty board had approved the plan and secrecy was paramount.

Keyes' plan had been well received by Admiral Jellicoe who now requested Bacon to return the papers. Bacon agreed to bring them to London within a day or two. Jellicoe endorsed the two blocking operations but awaited any suggestions from Bacon. A week later, an officer from the Plans Department went to Dover, where Bacon acknowledged he was in favour of the attack but in a different manner. He visited the Admiralty on 18 December where he discussed at length the plan. Throughout the meeting, he derided the unsupported usage of block ships. Instead, he preferred the use of two monitors and one infantry battalion, prior to the block ships' arrival. One monitor arriving in advance of the block ships was to land the infantry on the seaward side of the Mole, allowing the troops to storm the seaward end batteries. The other monitor was to enter the harbour in order to bombard the lock gates. The Admiralty Board accepted this proposal then granted Bacon permission to implement preparations for the attack. Keyes disliked the idea of bombarding the lock gates, but considered the use of storming parties a 'brilliant' idea. He did, however, protest against the involvement of the Army, for he preferred the operation to be a purely naval affair. He implored the use of bluejackets and marines for the storming parties. Their use would allow the opportunity for volunteers from the Grand Fleet to emulate their Army brothers in arms.

Within the navy it was felt sufficient volunteers would present them-

Royal Navy bluejackets in landing dress.

selves for such an operation. Jellicoe supported Keyes' amendment; a couple of days later Keyes travelled to the Grand Fleet to ask Admiral Beatty for the required men.

Towards the end of November the Channel Barrage Committee produced their first report; it was depressing news. The Naval Intelligence Department reported within the past ten months 253 U-boats had passed through the Dover straits, nearly all on the surface at night. The committee agreed with Keyes' previous proposal for an illuminated minefield; a weakness that had yet to be redressed. By mid December, Bacon had failed to implement illuminating the minefield, through which in the last fortnight twenty-nine submarines had journeyed on the surface.

The First Sea Lord lost his patience; on 15 December he ordered the Dover Patrol to concentrate on the specific task of closing the straits to U-boats. Against the wishes of Bacon, the patrol craft were to scour the area with their searchlights, making the brightly lit ships vulnerable to

"The hideous crew of a U-boat." [Their caption not mine!]

counter-attack. Once discovered the submarine would have to dive for cover into the minefield and inevitably face destruction. Flares and searchlights were first used over the minefield on 20 December; that night *U59* was detected on the surface. The U-boat crash-dived to evade capture but struck a mine. Her loss also sealed the fate of Admiral Bacon, for Keyes' criticism now seemed justifiable.

Shortly before Christmas, at a meeting of the Admiralty chiefs, Jellicoe refused a proposal for a change of command for the Dover patrol. Following the meeting, Sir Eric Geddes paid a visit to the King, who agreed to the change at the Admiralty. The following day Admiral Jellicoe resigned, to be succeeded next day by Sir Rosslyn Wemyss. A few days later Keyes was summoned to meet Wemyss; immediately Keyes entered the room he said, 'Well Roger, you have talked a hell of a lot about what ought to be done in the Dover area. Now you must go down there and prove it all yourself.' The removal of Bacon was personally embarassing but, gracious in defeat, he suggested an immediate changeover. On New Year's Day, the now Vice-Admiral Keyes took command of the Dover Patrol. Initially he met with hostility from his subordinate officers whose loyalty remained with the deposed, but much respected, Admiral Bacon. Keyes opened the admiral's safe and then produced copies of the *U59* documents. It came as quite a shock to the officers when Keyes also announced ninety-five per cent of submarines were by-passing the net defences. His sincerity won over his new staff, who until then firmly believed the Germans were avoiding the Straits. The entire Dover Patrol was rapidly revolutionised, patrols doubled and the minefield, due to the ingenuity of a certain Wing Commander Brock, was, according to Winston Churchill, 'as brightly lit as Piccadilly Circus'.

In January, the net barrage and patrol ships claimed several U-boats. The Germans responded on 14 February when enemy destroyers took advantage of a chaotic breakdown in signal communications. Under cover of darkness they attacked eight trawlers, damaged a paddle minesweeper and a drifter, before slipping away unmolested. Keyes was aghast to discover eighty-nine officers and auxiliary crew members were killed; an additional thirty were wounded. After a court of enquiry, three naval officers were relieved of command for failing to engage the enemy.

The Admiralty believed significant numbers of U-boats were operating from the 'Kapersnest' or Pirates' Lair. Continuous day and night bombing raids by aircraft failed to make the ports inoperable; indeed the lock gate at Zeebrugge was reputed to have a charmed existence. A major naval bombardment was not an option for the shore-based batteries stood a much greater chance of hitting a three-hundred foot long British warship, than the latter had of destroying an encased gun position. As the army failed to break out of the Ypres Salient, bogged down in the mud of Passchendaele in the autumn of 1917, a naval blocking operation became the only real option.

Throughout the distinguished history of the Royal Navy [or any other], no block ship had successfully completed its task. During the Russian-Japanese war, for example, the Japanese made three attempts to block Port Arthur. Eighteen block ships were used, but not one was scuttled in the correct position. The Admiralty appreciated the slim odds of success but resolved to discover a countermeasure to each major problem. They succeeded, but it was still a mission born out of desperation and necessity.

Notes

[1] For example the old tramp steamer *Lodorer*, renamed *Farnborough* was armed with five twelve-pounders and two six-pounders.

[2] He was killed on the night of 17/18 November 1941. As a Temporary Lieutenant Colonel [11 Scottish Commando] he penetrated 250 miles behind the lines to attack the Libyan Head Quarters and residence of Field Marshal Rommel. After he and two others gained entry to the residence, Keyes was killed. He already wore the MC for leadership in Syria, and the *Croix de Guerre* for conspicuous merit at Narvik. On two previous occasions, one of his forebears had been unsuccessfully nominated for a VC.

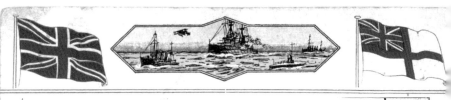

WHAT THE BRITISH NAVY IS DOING.
A reply to the Pessimist.

What is the British Navy doing?
  We have the right to ask,
In this mighty war that's being waged,
  Do they fulfil their task?
Now tell me pray! What have they done?
  Why don't they show some fight,
And fetch the German warships out
  From Heligoland Bight?
Now listen! my pessimistic friend,
  In a few short lines I'll tell
How our Navy's doing splendid work,
  And do their duty well.
Our ships are manned with gallant men,
  The bravest and the best,
They keep from off our shores the foe,
  While we in safety rest.
'Tis true the pirates sink some ships,
  But the toll grows less each day,

Because our gallant sailor men,
  Are always under weigh.
Thousands of British merchantmen
  Now sail the ocean main
With commerce, goods of every sort,
  Then back to port again.
Did e'er such armies cross the seas,
  A grand and noble band!
Our Navy makes it possible,
  That they in safety land;
And when they're called upon to fight
  They'll show their metal true,
And fight as only British can,
  Our noble lads in blue,
Stand to their guns that thunder forth
  And show in that dread hour,
How the enemy doth fear and shake,
  'Neath the British Navy's power.

Published by E. CARTER, St. George's Road, Weybridge.   Copyright.

38

Chapter Three

OPERATION ZO

Keyes and his staff immediately began work on the logistics of attacking the Belgian coast and sealing the port entrances. Two simultaneous operations using concrete-filled light cruisers to block both harbours, each defended by batteries of the heaviest calibre, reflected the dire situation of the Nation. At Zeebrugge, Royal Marine and naval storming parties would attack the Mole in a purely diversionary attack, to draw fire away from the approaching block ships.

The object of the hazardous operation was to deny to the enemy for an indefinite period the use of his advanced bases at Bruges and his refuge at Ostend. If successful this would immobilise some forty or fifty submarines berthed or refitting at both locations on the night of the attack.

The planning was meticulous; it needed to be for 168 [including eight monitors] craft of every shape and size fulfilling different roles were involved. Their movements across over sixty miles of open water had to be executed in accordance to a strict timetable. The revised plan was finalised and sanctioned by the Admiralty Board on the proviso the armada had to be ready to sail by 8 April. Time was of the essence; Keyes had four weeks to prepare his forlorn hope.

Gun at the entrance of the Mole.

The *Deutschland* Battery also known as *Jacobinessen* Battery was the most powerful battery on the Belgian Coast. Her four 15" guns bombared Dunkirk. Notice the two figures near the breach.

To achieve their aims the armada would have to deal with a series of hazards before reaching their objectives. Extensive mine-fields surrounded the Belgian coastline; to sweep a channel through these would take too long, also such activity would have alerted the enemy. During the sea passage the task force risked being sighted by German destroyers, aircraft or submarines; if sighted they would lose the element of surprise. The crossing required a dark night for cover; unfortunately, the darkness would make the locating of the harbours devoid of lighthouses or reliable navigation buoys extremely difficult. A natural hazard was the constantly shifting shoal waters; all available charts were obsolete as the Belgian coastal waters had not been surveyed for four years. The Flemish coast had a formidable mass of guns; the *Deutschland* and *Leugenboom* batteries had a range of thirty miles and fired a shell weighing a ton. The Germans had an accurate series of ranges; they could concentrate their fire on any point, and were capable of lighting up the sea as far as the horizon by star shells. The entrance to Zeebrugge harbour was closed by a boom formed by large stone-filled lighters and underwater nets. To enter the harbour the block ships would have to follow a narrow channel in front of the lighthouse, passing six 3.5 inch or 4 inch guns on the Mole extension at a range of one hundred yards. These were capable of firing through 360 degrees and could keep a vessel under fire from the moment it was seen until it reached the canal entrance. There were also three 5.9

inch guns at the extreme east end of the Mole proper. The ships would also draw fire from every gun mounted on the shore and canal jetties. A high tide was required for the block ships to obstruct the channel. The fleet was to arrive under cover of a man-made fog; for this cloak of invisibility to be effective a north or north-east wind was required to ensure a serviceable smokescreen, whilst any rain would prevent aircraft cover. The returning fleet had to be beyond range of the enemy artillery before daylight; to ensure this they had to leave their objective two hours before sunrise. On paper, this appears daunting; in reality it was an extremely hazardous mission from which few of its gallant participants expected to return.

The mouth of the Zeebrugge canal entrance had sand banks on both banks; large vessels could only pass along a dredged 120 feet wide central channel. Across this bottleneck, one or more block ships laden with concrete were to be scuttled athwart the flow of the channel. Belgian refugee engineers were consulted over the most effective position to sink the block ships. As the Admiralty was more used to sailing ships than scuttling them, it sought the opinions of leading salvage contractors regarding counter salvage measures. The answer was to line the hull of the block ships with concrete; this would increase the vessels' dead weight and ensure oxy-acetylene cutting torches could not be used for slicing up the ships. To prevent any patches being fixed onto the hulls each vessel was to have her keel blown out; the ship would sink quickly, hopefully in an upright position. Once settled on the bottom her ruptured keel would be inaccessible to the salvage team. Any attempt to dynamite

The concrete German submarine shelter at Bruges.

One of two lengthy cantilever submarine shelters (*Kragunterstaden*) in the Groot Handelsdok [Great trade dock].

the ships into more easily recovered sections would scatter the steel work. Each piece of debris would gather an accumulation of silt and contribute to a reduction in the channel depth. The height of the hull needed to be

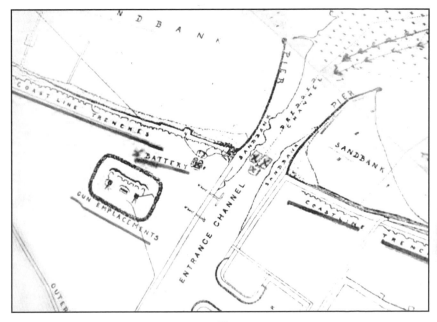

of a dimension capable of preventing vessels from passing over the wreck at high water.

The block ships had to be capable of sailing under their own steam, as the task of towing a block ship into a hostile port was impractical. Her draught [depth of hull in the water] could not be excessive due to the depth of the channel and the hazard of mines. She also had to have some defensive capabilities. Three old cruisers – HMS *Thetis*, *Intrepid*, and *Iphigenia*, commanded respectively by Commander Sneyd, Lieutenant Stuart S. Bonham Carter and Lieutenant Ivan Franks were to block the Zeebrugge canal. Two similar warships, HMS *Brilliant* and *Sirius*, commanded respectively by Commander A.E. Godsal and Lieutenant Commander H.N. Hardy, were to scuttle between the piers at Ostend. A third vessel, HMS *Vindictive*, was originally destined for Ostend; instead, she became the Zeebrugge assault ship. Each obsolete vessel displaced from 3,400 to 3,600 tons.

Two auxiliary craft proved more difficult to source; Captain Herbert C.J. Grant toured the nation's harbours without success until he arrived on the River Mersey. In 1907, Wallasey Corporation had taken delivery of the *Iris* and *Daffodil* at a cost of twenty thousand pounds each. They were wonderfully navigable and amongst the swiftest and most powerful

HMS *Vindictive* before the raid.

Demonstration of Brock's patent fog-producing apparatus on board *Daffodil.* **(below)**

of their kind. Each was capable of carrying 1,675 passengers, they were 155 feet long, had a 41 feet beam, were flat bottomed and drew only seven feet of water. One of the ferries had survived a collision when an enormous gash had split her hull to the waterline. Her twin hull saved her although her compartments were flooded. She remained buoyant; laden with a thousand passengers she safely wallowed her way to the shore. Grant recognised their potential for pushing the *Vindictive* alongside the Mole; they were also capable of delivering or rescuing a large body of men. Their shallow draft allowed them to pass over minefields or torpedoes.

On Sunday 12 February, Capt. W.H. Fry (Wallasey Ferries' manager) was informed that the Admiralty were to take two of his boats. When Fry reminded the Senior Staff officer that they already had two; (the officer had served with Fry on *Terrible*), the officer remarked, 'They were to save life.' 'In that case take the lot,' replied Fry. That night he went to London and in the First Lord's office he hazarded the remark that the boats were to land men at Zeebrugge. He received a blow in the back from his former comrade who urged him not to make guesses. Events, however, proved he was a good guesser.

44

The spaces around the ferries' fore and after ends were plated-in for protection and sundry other alterations were effected at Cammel Lairds' Birkenhead shipyard. Two Wallasey Ferry engineers then accompanied *Iris* and *Daffodil* to Portsmouth; none of the civilian crews were involved in the raid. At Portsmouth, the vessels' conversion continued with the accoutrements of war. *Iris* carried a Stokes mortar on the forward part of her main deck, a Vickers machine gun protruded from a sandbagged position on the port wheelhouse and another remained in reserve on the upper deck. Marine Private Holdridge operated the weapon on *Iris*. Davits for grappling irons, scaling ladders and revolutionary smoke apparatus were fitted.

This smoke was an artificial fog developed especially for the operation by Wing Commander Frank Arthur Brock, RNAS. He was an expert in pyrotechnics for he was the son of the founder of Brock's fireworks, and a factory director. The ingenious Brock was tasked with inventing a man-made fog to provide cover for the Operation Zeebrugge Ostend task force. A special buoy was also required that would automatically light up when placed in water; Brock designed and delivered this prototype within twenty-four hours. This inventor had already developed an incendiary bullet for destroying Zeppelins; he was responsible for inventing and successfully illuminating the Channel anti-submarine defences. During the Second World War RAF pathfinders illuminated targets with flares invented by Brock. Within the secret fog factory which Brock had started at Dover, he and his sixty-man team designed and developed a smoke apparatus devoid of a telltale flame, also other novel gadgets. A key ingredient used was saxin, a substitute for sugar, much in demand by diabetics. All available supplies were diverted to Brock's smoke workshops; it was yet another food shortage for those with unsweetened tea to grumble about.

Wing Commander Frank A. Brock, RNAS.

They installed smoke apparatus on the larger vessels but the all-important smokescreen would emanate from a flotilla of over thirty motor launches. A further eighteen coastal motor boats were to inject whatever mayhem they could deliver. Keyes was originally to direct the operation from the *Vindictive*, but as this would isolate him from his other vessels he had his flag in the destroyer *Warwick*. On board the destroyer he could roam the area, keep in touch with components of the force and make on the spot decisions. Keyes' huge white ensign, of

45

The destroyer HMS *Phoebe*.

proportions suitable for flying from a battleship, would fly from the mast of *Warwick*; nobody could mistake the command ship. A dozen other destroyers were organised in units. Unit L was *Phoebe* and *North Star*. Unit M was *Trident* and *Mansfield*. Unit R comprised *Velox*, *Melpomeme*, *Moorsom* and *Morris*. Unit X was *Tempest* and *Tetrach*. A separate aiding and covering force would also guard the rear and flanks to prevent the force being caught unaware by enemy vessels returning to port.

HMS *Vindictive*, a second-class cruiser, was launched in December 1897. She was capable of twenty knots, measured 320 feet long and displaced 5,750 tons. Parts of her deck had only one inch of armour plate. She came out of retirement to serve as the assault ship of the bluejackets and marines who were to storm the Mole. She was not Keyes' preferred choice as he would have preferred a large passenger steamer with a shallow draught and tall superstructure but no such vessel was available. *Vindictive* was the right size but she drew nineteen feet; it would be curtains if she sailed into an unexpected minefield. At Chatham *Vindictive* took on an appearance like no other warship; her large masts disappeared, as did some of her guns. A mast section mounted across her deck protruded past her hull to act as a bumper when she came alongside the Mole. To assist the storming parties to reach the Mole, a special upper deck was constructed along her port side, with wide ramps leading to it from the starboard side. Along the edge of this upper deck, the shipyard carpenters constructed eighteen narrow hinged drawbridge-style gangways just wide enough to take a man. Once alongside, these gangways would drop onto the Mole parapet allowing the raiders to dash ashore. Along the port side, lengths of twelve-inch square timber were fitted as buffers, supplemented with vast hazelwood fenders.

A mushroom-shaped fighting top, equipped with two oil-fired flamethrowers invented by Brock, Lewis guns and pompoms capable of laying fire on to the Mole, was constructed on the stump of her forward mast. Her fore and after naval guns were replaced by 7.5 inch howitzers and amidships behind the rear funnel was an eleven inch howitzer, assorted weaponry completing her very unseaman-like transformation. One of her new crew remarked 'Well it's darned good to be on board a blessed something, but I am blowed if I know what she is.'

Inside Chatham dockyard, the old cruisers designated as block ships underwent conversion. Engine rooms and other vulnerable areas were protected with rubble and concrete. Salvage experts advised on the best anti-recovery positions to place concrete ballast. Each of the block ships was to have a series of mines positioned on the

The fighting top on *Vindictive* where Sergeant Finch earned his VC.

hull bottom, designed to rip the bottom out of the vessel, swiftly sinking her in the canal entrance. As Germany was desperately short of copper and brass, any redundant fittings were removed. Duplicate conning and steering appeared, swathed in shrapnel-proof matting. Every ton of material removed was replaced with Portland cement, positioned two feet above the keel to thwart any salvage attempt.

The landing brows (or gangways) fitted on the assault ship *Vindictive*.

The conversion of the block ships.

An amendment to the original plan was the inclusion of submarines *C1* and *C3* built in 1906 and 1907. One thousand men defended the Mole and canal and to prevent hostile reinforcements advancing along the Mole the viaduct had to be severed. Each submarine, manned by a skeleton crew of two officers and four men, would be rammed into the viaduct and **C3 and her crew leaving harbour with a regular crew complement.**

explode their cargo of high explosives. As they neared the target, the crew were to set delay time fuses and make good their escape. Each submarine carried two motor-skiffs and a light scaling ladder as a means of escape to the viaduct if other equipment failed.

While the surface vessels were being adapted the recruitment of personnel commenced; Keyes had to pick his commanders with care for each man would need a cool and resourceful nature with the heart of a lion. The selection and training of officers and men was even more important than the selection of vessels. Each naval officer was well acquainted with Keyes; he chose men whom he knew were dependable, not his favourites as some make out. They in turn offered to their men the opportunity to embark on an undisclosed but hazardous mission. There was no shortage of willing hands wishing to break the monotony of naval routine. The personnel required for the block ships, assault vessels and for other special purposes, amounted to eighty-six officers and 1,698 men; the latter figure included some 740 men from the Royal Marines.

Due to the civil unrest in Ireland, in November 1917 an extra battalion of marines was raised. This new battalion comprised a company of Royal Marine Artillery [RMA] and one from each of the Royal Marine Light Infantry [RMLI] Divisions. Although intended for duties in Ireland, the

Five Platoon, 4/Royal Marine Light Infantry, with Lieutenant Cooke.

49

battalion instead supplied officers and men for the general draft. As the plans for Zeebrugge and Ostend evolved, the proposals for involving the marines were discussed on 11 January 1918 by the First Lord, the First Sea Lord, and the Adjutant General Royal Marines. As a result, orders were issued cancelling all further drafts from the battalion. Three RMLI companies were to be completed to strength, placed under the command of Lieutenant Colonel Chichester and then trained at various headquarters. This officer transpired to be medically unfit; Major B.H. Elliot DSO took command. From within the Royal Marines Detachments of the Grand Fleet came two officers and fifty men of the RMA; these were formed into a trench mortar section. A further two officers and eighty men from the RMLI[1] were absorbed into companies of their divisions. The orders for raising the battalion were issued on 6 February 1918 and to preserve secrecy it was claimed the battalion was to be attached to the Royal Naval Division in France for a specific operation.

Almost every major ship in the Grand Fleet provided participants for the raid, as did HMAS *Australia* berthed at Rosyth after convoy escort duty between Bergen and Aberdeen. From her crew Warrant Officer Artificer Engineer W. Edgar, five seamen and four stokers were assigned to the raid – choice was not an option.

One of the British seamen was nineteen-year-old W. Wainwright, who had joined the Royal Navy when aged sixteen. He served on board *Monarch* at the Battle of Jutland and was then drafted to *Superb* in 1917. He described his recruitment for the mission.

The early days of February 1918 found me a minute cog in the machinery of the greatest armada known, The Grand Fleet – a seaman on board the *Superb*, stationed in the melancholy regions of Scapa Flow. One evening, in the midst of our usual festivities, namely looking mournful at each other, Nemesis in the shape of a large overfed crusher [ships' police] overtook me. He informed me that a large piece of 'Gold Braid' living an exclusive life at the far end of the ship had become interested in me, and would I favour him with an interview?

I followed the pompous "body snatcher", along brightly lit passages; feeling dismayed, but on reaching the Commander's cabin all fears were dispelled. I was cordially invited to enter and

Lieutenant Colonel Bertram H. Elliot, DSO, RMLI.

found myself in a circle consisting of the Commander, Secretary, Master-at-Arms, and five able seamen, all wearing a vacant expression.

With my arrival, a full quota appeared to be made up, as the Commander rose to his feet and produced a paper, informed us that the Commander in Chief had sent a signal for six seamen, for special service.

He went on to say that, not knowing what the stunt was, he could not give the least idea, except that it was dangerous work. The chances were nine out of ten that we should "snuff it", and we should be under twenty-three, single, physically fit, and able to use a revolver and oar. From the conditions it appeared as though the result of the war rested on us, oil was poured on troubled waters with phrases of honour and glory. After letting his words sink in he gazed at the condemned six, and stated that if they did not want to volunteer nothing would be said and the men could just carry on.

However, no one moved, and no doubt thinking that I looked the silliest pigeon there, the Commander asked if I would go? Having served a miserable six months in that ship, and my third year in that dismal theatre of war, I informed him promptly I would be glad of it.

To get away from his tender care was an ambition of mine. Needless to say the remaining five jumped at the idea, and we were beamed on with pride, solemnly shaken by the hand and called heroes.

With their new hero status, the 'condemned six' were spared the pleasures of scrubbing *Superb*'s wooden decks, for they were to work no more on that ship.

Morning saw us step off in fine style, in athletic garb, led by a high stepping physical training instructor and watched by an admiring and cynical crowd. We were kept at it all the afternoon, our only respite being the ju jitsu lesson. Later we landed for revolver practice, wandering around a deserted island and practising drawing and shooting. As the days went on, we grew into whalebone and whipcord, thanks to the slave-driver who took us in his care.

From throughout the Grand Fleet 200 hand-picked sailors were recruited, each small unit undergoing similar training as Wainwright's group, before being ordered south. Before leaving their ship, they were permitted several days' leave to say farewell to their relatives. For many this would be their final goodbye. At the conclusion of their leave, the sailors joined the depot ship *Hindustan* at Chatham. Wainwright wrote:

51

Holborn station presented a curious spectacle, groups of seamen could be seen walking with suppressed excitement and looking questioningly at anyone wearing the ribbon of some ship in the Grand Fleet. The Chatham train drew all these adventurers into its compartments and here the question, "Are you in this stunt and what is it going to be?" was freely debated, but no one could throw any light on the subject. Whoever had organised the whole business had preserved its secrecy in no uncertain fashion.

Throughout March the three companies of bluejackets and the marines

Private Edwin [Eddy] Lankshear, RMLI. He was born in Bermondsey in 1900 and joined the RMLI in 1917. His brother Frank flew in an RE8 as an observer during the battle of Passchendaele, was mortally wounded and died in August 1917. Within the marines, he acquired the nickname 'Dick'. Like most veterans of his era, he seldom talked of his war experiences except on one occasion. 'We sailed in old *Vindictive*. We got alongside the Mole and they ran out the landing ramps under intense enemy fire. I dashed ashore carrying a Lewis gun, which was so heavy I could not use it to return fire, until I was ashore with a support to rest it on. We lost a great deal of good men, but eventually we heard the signal to retire, and the old ship took us quickly out of danger.'
Dick fought on the Western Front and in Russia throughout the Vladivostok, Murmansk and Archangel Campaign. He went on the 1923 Empire world cruise in HMS *Danae*. He completed twelve years' service in 1929. During the Second World War, he volunteered as an ARP driver. In 1966 he emigrated to Australia, where he died in 1971.

were rigorously trained in grenade, bayonet fighting, demolition and trench raiding. The marines trained under the personal supervision of Lieutenant Colonel Elliot DSO. As second in command of the naval forces in Serbia, Elliot had received the DSO.

They practised tactics day and night on a full size replica of the Mole, constructed from details supplied from aerial photographs. Strips of canvas were laid out on Freedown at Deal, representing a drained canal bed accessed by an imaginary fifteen-foot drop (representing the Mole parapet to the quay wall). Officers commanding units were ordered to 'Imbue their commands with the idea of carrying the operation through with the bayonet; rifle fire, machine-gun fire and bomb throwing were only to be resorted to when necessary to break down enemy resistance'. The raiders' role was falsely described as 'a mopping up and consolidating of the position occupied by an enemy advanced munitions dump and store depot and holding the same during the time necessary for specially detailed Royal Engineers to prepare the various points for demolition; when the object is accomplished the battalion will be withdrawn'.

The marine artillerymen selected for operating the howitzers trained at Shoeburyness, the Stokes mortar crews underwent tuition at Deal. The raiding personnel were split into three distinct groups; Major Elliot commanded the fourth battalion marine storming party. Captain Henry C. Halahan DSO had served for most of the war in command of the naval guns on the Northern Front and within range of the enemy guns for three years. He was to command the naval storming party, comprising six officers and 150 men split into three groups. Two would sail on *Vindictive*, the third on *Iris*. Halahan was the senior naval officer on board *Vindictive*. As the Senior Executive Officer, he would normally have been responsible for the handling of the mother ship, but Alfred Carpenter had the great responsibility of safely navigating *Vindictive* to the Mole but was of lesser rank than Halihan. To prevent any difficulty arising from this unusual situation, Halihan generously proposed his acting rank of captain be transferred to Carpenter. By doing so, he became junior to Carpenter, but his sole aim was for the success of the mission. On board *Iris* there would be a combined unit of fifty seamen

Captain Henry C. Halahan, DSO, RN. KIA on the *Vindictive*.

53

and twenty-two marines, which comprised the demolition party under Lieutenant Commander Cecil C. Dickinson, RN.

The 4th Battalion Royal Marine Light Infantry (4/RMLI) was to provide the officers and men of the storming force, the crews of four Stokes guns, one eleven inch howitzer, five pompoms, and some Lewis guns of the *Vindictive* armament. They were to reach Zeebrugge on board the *Vindictive*, excluding 'A' [Chatham] Company, two Vickers guns of the machine-gun section, and two Stokes guns, which sailed on board *Iris II* [throughout this work we refer to her as *Iris*. The navy already had an *Iris* in service].

Seaman Wainwright recorded:

During the next few days we formed into companies, platoons, and sections. We were introduced to our leaders and put through our paces on St. Mary's Island both day and night. We were then handed over to the instructors of the fifth and sixth Middlesex Regiment, to be polished off and to be instructed in the fine arts of land warfare. The weeks that passed then were one mass of bayonet drill, pointing and parrying, blob sticks, bombs, trench mortars, gas, night attacks, final assaults, and musketry, and we were gradually becoming excellent soldiers. A change in the run of things found our section transferred into a three-inch Stokes trench mortar battery. We were armed with a combination of nautical weapons, the pistol and cutlass (the latter article is only useful for deck cricket, when three of them make good wickets), and our training regarding the wielding of this barbarous weapon began again. The worst punishment a man could be threatened with was

The ferry *Iris* in wartime livery; this is a post-raid photograph. Notice the damage.

expulsion from the party.

A further rumour circulated claiming the practice ground represented a defended area near Calais, which would require capturing by the navy in connection with a blocking operation in Calais. This seemed wholly credible as on 21 March Ludendorff had launched a devastating spring offensive; the British front lines retracted before this formidable onslaught. Ultimately, the German waves were repulsed but, in the meantime, the pressure on the Royal Navy to launch a strike intensified.

Our training was now nearing completion, and our massed attacks were taking on a sameness, which pointed at some concerted item we were rehearsing for. Many inventions were tried, with a view to saving as many lives as possible and we had practically reached the acme of perfection and were in danger of going stale. One morning about this period, our usual route was changed, and we found ourselves in the Royal Marine Barracks. After being thumped, patted and pushed around by a rotund sergeant-major, we emerged into fresh air, in a dazed state and a khaki uniform.

Seaman W. Wainwright.

For the raid, each member of the shore parties wore khaki uniform under

Private Eddie Grayken, RMLI. This veteran of Zeebrugge joined the RMLI in May 1913. He went on to serve in *Irresistible*, followed by *Europa*, in 1915. At the Dardanelles, he escaped from two torpedoed ships. In 1916 he hung his hammock in *Implacable*, but in 1917, joined *Exmouth*, the Portsmouth Division and *Attentive II*. He volunteered from the latter posting to participate in the Zeebrugge raid on board *Iris*. During the action, due to a backfiring gun, he sustained splintered bones in his face. After the war, he gained employment as a steward on board a passenger ship and jumped ship in America. His new life in the young and exciting country came to an abrupt end due to his war wounds, as he had to return home for specialist treatment. Eddie was one of the last fifty members of the Zeebrugge Association whose lapel badge he constantly wore. He died in 1976. Today his grandson proudly wears the badge of the amiable veteran.

which he wore a primitive life belt. All wore leather boots minus the regulation steel studs on the soles, to mask their approach! A steel helmet, gas respirator, sixty rounds of ammunition and Mills bombs completed the ensemble. Each platoon was equipped with a flamethrower and Lewis gun, also two ladders and four ropes for the descent from the parapet; heavy scaling ladders were also provided.

On 6 April, the marines boarded the train for Dover, where they boarded the transport *Royal Edward*, destination unknown. When the vessel was no longer visible from the shore, the portly *Daffodil* [officially named *Daffodil IV* while in Admiralty service] arrived alongside. The puzzled marines then clambered aboard the ferry. The ruse was all part of operational secrecy; instead of crossing the Channel the marines' ferry altered course. The key vessels in the armada were now riding the tide on the Swin, an anchorage at the mouth of the Thames estuary; on arriving at this isolated spot, the marines disembarked into the depot ship

HMS *Hindustan*.

Hindustan, but due to insufficient room C Company was assigned to *Vindictive*. The following day the blanket of secrecy lifted when the true mission objective was revealed. Clay scale models were produced, supported by aerial photographs; the gathered raiders were stunned by the boldness of the scheme. They remained undaunted despite their slim chances of surviving the assault, for at best they might become a prisoner of war. The briefing was comprehensive for if high casualties were sustained every man knew the job in hand and could press home the attack. From this point, no further communication was permitted with the shore.

The task force was ready; all that was required was a combination of suitable weather, tide and darkness. The first possible date was 9 April, but a severe southerly wind made the sea conditions unfavourable. Two days later the conditions were ideal; late in the afternoon, in strict adherence to the meticulously planned timetable, the fleet of 160 vessels sailed for the rendezvous at the Goodwin Sands. By early evening three columns of ships steamed eastwards. *Vindictive* had *Iris* and *Daffodil* in tow, for their range was too short to complete the return journey. Other vessels towed the smaller craft, also the specially prepared submarines. Several buoys had been laid at predetermined points; as the fleet approached each marker they synchronised their positions with the pre-ordained timetable. Everything was going exactly to plan and hopes were running high. Meanwhile Dunkirk-based bomber aircraft from 65th Royal Air Force squadron carried out a preliminary bombardment. To ensure the skeleton crews arrived fresh at their destination, each of the block ships carried thirty extra stokers. At the final buoy, these were to transfer to a Dover-bound minelayer.

During preparations this planned disembarking of stokers led to a slight insurrection on board *Intrepid*. Several men demanded to see the Captain; when ordered to explain themselves the leader said 'Me and my mates understands as how some of the crew have to leave the ship on the way across to Zeebruggy. The Master at Arms says it's us lot and we aren't going to leave.' The Captain explained they would be too many to rescue and would jeopardise the rescue boat, but the men stood their ground. No doubt bowing to their fighting spirit their Captain agreed to take a spare gun crew and ordered the mutineers to draw lots for the honour.

Before the ships got underway again, the weather conspired against the raiders, for the gentle wind blowing towards the coast changed direction; the wind was now unfavourable for the all-important smokescreen. Keyes'

Submarine *C3* in tow.

57

fleet was a frustrating ninety minutes from their objective but he had no other alternative than to signal 'return to base'. *Coastal Motor Boat 33 (CMB 33)* failed to return.

Korvettenkapitan Eric E. Schultze, a member of staff of Admiral von Schroeder, wrote:

> *During the unsuccessful attempt on the foregoing night between April 12th and 13th, of which at first we did not understand the purport, a heavily damaged English motor boat ran aground to the east of Ostend. In this boat we found a map giving us first hand information concerning the plan of the expedition, it was the English naval chart number 124 "Ostend Roads"; written in black ink was the inscription "Number 33 Boat Chart April 9th 1918". This map indicated the course to be steered with full explanations such as block ships approach. It was not difficult for us to draw the necessary conclusions for Zeebrugge.*

How *CMB33* became captured remains a mystery.[2]

On Sunday 14 April, the last day of the 'possible period', the weather appeared suitable and the flotilla sailed. Two hours later, due to rising tide and wind, Keyes again signalled for the ships to return to port. This was a devastating blow for Keyes as this was apparently his last chance of an April attack. The rudimentary living accommodation on *Hindustan* was considered detrimental to the morale of the men; *Dominion* arrived to ease the over-crowding. The waiting was exerting a great strain on all ranks; games and exercises were started, and all attempts were made to

The wreck of *CMB 33*. The enemy pose for an enterprising postcard photographer.

keep the men fit. The solution would have been time ashore but the need to maintain secrecy prevented this.

Events on the Western Front were increasingly critical, for German forces continued to drive back the Allies. The Allied infantry, despite being overwhelmed by superior numbers and innovative tactics, fought bravely. Precious ground, steeped in the blood of their fallen comrades, fell to the advancing field grey troops. On 11 April, Sir Douglas Haig issued his now famous 'Backs to the wall' order. This order appears below in its entirety for it highlights the predicament upon the Western Front.

To all ranks of the British army in France and Flanders.

Three weeks ago today, the enemy began his terrific attacks against us on a fifty mile [eighty km] front. His objects are to separate us from the French, to take the Channel ports, and to destroy the British Army.

In spite of throwing already 106 divisions into the battle and enduring the most reckless sacrifice of human life, he has yet made little progress towards his goals. We owe this to the determined fighting and self-sacrifice of our troops.

Words fail me to express the admiration which I feel for the splendid resistance offered by all ranks of our army under the most trying circumstances. Many among us now are tired. To those I would say that victory will belong to the side which holds out the longest.

The French army is moving rapidly and in great force to our support. There is no other course open to us but to fight it out. Every position must be held to the last man; there must be no retirement. With our backs to the wall, and believing in the justice in our course each one of us must fight on to the end. The safety of our homes and the freedom of mankind depend alike upon the conduct of each one of us at this critical moment.

Meanwhile the Royal Navy still appeared to be doing little to ease the situation. The army appeared to be carrying the full burden of the war while the battleships and heavy cruisers of the navy appeared to be inactive.[3]

Keyes had always championed April as the ideal period to launch the attack as several high tides coincided with a moonless night. The next suitable period would not occur until mid May. The Admiralty now decided it was unwise to keep the assaulting parties indefinitely confined to the cramped accommodation on board the depot ships. The raid would be cancelled and all personnel returned to their units, the block ships would be paid off pending the breakers' yard. Undaunted Keyes pressed the Admiralty Board for fresh orders to attack between 22 and 26 April. He had always maintained a dark night was essential to the success of the operation. The raid would now occur in a period of a full moon yet, despite the lack of this fundamental requirement, he successfully pleaded his case. Keyes was desperate to complete his task; few doubted that whatever conditions Mother Nature offered this time he would go ahead come what may. It was now or never.

On 19 April Admiral von Capelle, Secretary for the German Navy, made a rousing speech in which he said:

> *Even the greatest pessimist must say that the position of our opponents is deteriorating rapidly, and that any doubt regarding the final success of the U-boat war is unjustified.*

Little did he know the Imperial German Navy would soon receive the biggest insult any navy could suffer.

Notes

[1] The Royal Marines proper formed on 22 June 1923, when the RMA and RMLI amalgamated. Throughout this work, unless specified, Royal Marine refers to either or both units.

[2] After the war, Sir Roger Keyes and Captain Carpenter VC both published first-hand accounts of the raids; both authors omitted the loss of *CMB33*.

[3] During the Great War, the Royal Navy lost two dreadnoughts, three battle cruisers, eleven battleships, twenty-five cruisers, fifty-four submarines, sixty-four destroyers and ten torpedo boats. Total naval casualties were 34,642 dead and 4,510 wounded.

Chapter Four

THE ZEEBRUGGE RAID

After anxious days of waiting on 22 April the fickle weather hinted it might be favourable for an attack. The fleet prepared to sail at 5 p.m.; during that afternoon, while walking down to the harbour with her husband, Eva Keyes reminded him the next morning would be St. George's Day and implored him to use 'St. George for England' as his battle cry. The first vessel to leave was the monitor *Erubus* which, accompanied by other monitors, would carry out their usual long-range bombardment of Zeebrugge. Monitors for a similar role off Ostend departed from Dunkirk at 8.35 p.m., and a force of destroyers under the command of Sir Reginald Tywhitt sailed from Harwich to provide cover against a surprise enemy attack from the sea. A total of forty-seven vessels, including nine French torpedo craft and motor launches, sailed from Dunkirk.

The concentration of the force occurred in daylight near the Goodwin Sands. Once again the force headed eastwards in three columns. Leading the centre column was *Vindictive*, towing behind her the tubby *Iris* and *Daffodil*. In her wake steamed the five block ships. At the head of the starboard column *Warwick*, flying Keyes' enormous white ensign, preceded two destroyers. The latter vessels were to safeguard *Vindictive* from hostile destroyer attack as she lay vulnerable alongside the Mole. Astern submarines *C1* and *C3* were in tow astern of the destroyers *Trident* and *Mansfield*. The port column comprised destroyers; in between the columns were two dozen coastal motor boats (*CMB*s) and over sixty motor launches, all manned by volunteer crews. Some of these small craft were to race into Zeebrugge harbour to torpedo the enemy destroyers before they could put to sea. Others were to act as rescue boats for the block ship crews, or lay smokescreens. Lieutenant James Dawbarn Young, RNVR, in command of *ML 110*, had volunteered for the most hazardous task of all. His tiny boat was to precede the block ships and light the harbour and canal entrance with Brock's calcium buoys.

The badge of the Zeebrugge Association.

Shortly before nightfall, Keyes sent by semaphore the now legendary signal 'St. George for England'. Captain Carpenter in command of *Vindictive* replied 'May we give the dragon's tail a damned good twist'.

The full moon made it almost as bright as day; visibility was considered to be ten miles. One of Keyes' officers remarked 'But there is one thing about it, even if the enemy expects us, they will never think we could be such fools as to try to pull it off on a night like this.'

Perhaps St. George was listening, for the weather suddenly became misty, reducing visibility to less than a mile. Clouds obscured the moon and a steady drizzle began. Although the elements were now in the fleet's favour, the rain and low cloud prevented any aircraft cover.

It was now pitch dark, for the clouds had obscured the moon. The final buoy (position G) located sixteen miles from Zeebrugge was reached by 10.00 p.m. Here the surplus crews were to transfer to *Lingfield*, a Dover-bound minesweeper, but many of them on board *Thetis* and *Iphigenia* hid, for they did not intend to miss the action. As commendable as the stowaways' actions were, their numbers hampered the motor launches' rescue of the block ship crews. The craft assigned to collect the surplus crew on *Intrepid* had a mishap; this saved her commander a potentially embarrassing situation with surplus crew who had already announced their intention to remain on board. This was also the parting of the ways for the separate legs of the operation. The Ostend force, including the block ships *Sirius* and *Brilliant*, set a course for a rendezvous north of Ostend. They were to come under the command of Commander Lynes, in charge of the Dunkirk flotilla. Both blocking operations were to be

Bunkers in the sand dunes. The coast bristled with defensive measures.

launched simultaneously. At Ostend the plan was simpler for it was a straightforward blocking operation. We shall concentrate on that operation in a following chapter.

The main attacking force then steamed for the almost impregnable enemy naval base. The coastal motor boats and submarines then cast off, to proceed under their own power. *Warwick* and *Whirlwind*, followed by the other destroyers, drew ahead on either bow to deal with any approaching enemy vessels. Monitors were slow moving warships, essentially a heavy gun turret mounted on a shallow drafted hull. Two such vessels, *Erebus* and *Terror*, guarded by three destroyers, took up position for the bombardment of Zeebrugge. During the operation, enemy shell fell close to the monitors, but neither was hit. When the *Vindictive* arrived at a position where she needed to alter course for the Mole, *Warwick*, *Phoebe* and *North Star* swung to starboard, and patrolled until the final phase of the withdrawal. Wainwright described the atmosphere on board *Vindictive* thus:

> We whiled away the time on the channel trip with impromptu concerts and dances and I doubt if any there thought of the serious mission of this strangely assorted fleet. After supper had been served, practically everybody snatched an hour or two's sleep before the fateful hour; how anyone could sleep with an adventure like the one before us speaks volumes for the mental and physical fitness of the party. Our slumbers were disturbed by a bugle call, and a ration of hot chicken broth was served out supplemented by a ration of grog, the latter being practically untouched, it being thought that a clear head and steady eye would be more beneficial.

At fifty minutes to zero hour the hawser towing *Iris* and *Daffodil* snapped and from here on they were on their own. The block ships now slackened speed, for they were to arrive at the Mole some twenty minutes later than *Vindictive*. At 11.30 p.m., the Blankenberge light buoy was spotted; this allowed the opportunity for a dead reckoning of their position. The small craft had in the meantime raised the smokescreen, running in close so the artificial fog they emitted and their constant movement hid them from the enemy. The roar of their engines alerted the enemy, their artillery commenced pumping shells into the artificial fog and star shells burst into the night sky for they realised something was amiss. The favourable wind died down, lessening the effect of the smokescreen. At four minutes before midnight the *Vindictive* emerged from the smokescreen, to find the Mole three hundred yards off the port bow. *Vindictive*'s telegraphs called for full speed ahead and altered course for the Mole. Incredulous German gunners blinked their eyes in amazement, briefly stunned into disbelief at the sight before their eyes.

Guns on the mole extension.

Sergeant Harry Wright, 10 Platoon Royal Marines, wrote:

We went up to get our men on the upper deck, into the darkness. Rifles were loaded and bayonets fixed. No lights were showing on any of the ships and everyone spoke in whispers. Our nerves were almost strained to breaking point. Would we get alongside the Mole without the Germans seeing us? There we stood shoulder to shoulder, rifles in hand ready for the dash forward. There was hardly a whisper, only the noise of the propellers breaking the water. Would we ever get there? 'Ah, what is that?' A star shell floated over the ship turning night into day, swiftly followed by another. 'They've seen us,' someone whispered. Then the silence was shattered by a terrific bang followed by a crash as fragments of shell flew amongst us, killing and maiming the brave fellows as they stood at their arms, crowded together thick as bees. The Mole was just in sight, we could see it off the port quarter, but it was too late. Our gunners replied to their fire but could not silence that terrible battery of five-inch guns firing into our ship at less than a range of 100 yards and from behind concrete walls.

The assault ship passed the Mole battery at an estimated distance of two hundred and fifty yards from the eastern gun, gradually lessening to fifty yards off the western gun. A petty officer attending a six inch gun on board *Vindictive* later stated that the range from the gun muzzle decreased to 'about three feet'! [Battleship gunners generally train over a fifteen-mile distance.] *Vindictive*'s port six inch battery, upper deck pompoms and the gun in the foretop instantly replied. A searchlight locked on the old cruiser, every available German gun now opened fire on her. She was due to come alongside almost opposite the fortified area on the seaward end of the Mole. Within five minutes, the *Vindictive* incurred tremendous damage to both the vessel and personnel.

As *Vindictive* bore down on the Mole all ranks were at their action

German barbed wire and shelters on the Mole.

stations, the storming parties obeyed orders to remain under cover until
the ship reached the Mole. Their senior officers however decided to take
up positions from where they could direct their men. Lieutenant Colonel
Bertram N. Elliot, DSO, and his second in command, Major Alexander
A. Cordner, the senior officers of the Royal Marine storming parties, took

Von Hindenburg, Von Schroeder and officers of the U-boat base of Flanders.

up a position on the bridge overlooking the gangway deck. Captain Henry C. Halahan, DSO, commanding the naval storming parties, with Commander Edwards RNVR beside him, were out on the exposed upper gangway deck. When the Mole battery roared into life in a few brief, minutes Elliot and Cordner were killed where they stood. Captain Halahan died and Commander Patrick Edwards lay wounded, shot in both legs.

Captain Chater had survived the explosion; after reporting their deaths to the commander of C Company the latter took command. The forward 7.5 inch howitzer crew were killed by the shell that killed the marine leader. A volunteer naval crew from a 6 inch gun took their place; while getting the gun ready a shell burst amongst them and all but two were killed or wounded. Acting Captain R. D. Brooks, RMA was in command of RMA gun detachments on board *Vindictive*; he not only led by example

The battered funnel of *Vindictive* dwarfs the two men.

but also commanded the crew of the 11 inch howitzer in its exposed position. Many other officers and men had broken cover as soon as the firing commenced; they had rushed up onto the upper deck, where they were scythed down by shrapnel and bullet.

At one minute past midnight on 23 April, St. George's Day *Vindictive* was alongside the Mole, precisely one minute behind schedule. With her vital hull and innards protected by the vast bulk of the Mole, only her upper works provided a target for German firepower; every few seconds projectiles of all calibres ripped into her steelwork.

Seaman Wainwright recalled the *Vindictive*'s arrival.

Every gun in the Vindictive *that could bear had now given tongue and the night was made hideous by the nerve-racking chatter of the pompoms, the deep bell-like boom of the howitzers and trench mortars,*

66

and the all pervading rattle of musketry and machine-gun fire; it
was hell with a vengeance and it seemed well-nigh miraculous that
human beings could live in such an inferno.

Against all the odds, *Vindictive* reached the Mole, arriving alongside in
a great tidal surge produced by her increased speed. Unfortunately she
overshot her intended position by approximately four hundred yards in
the shore direction. Instead of berthing alongside the battery, *Vindictive*
lay alongside number three shed. In peacetime, the vessel could have
repositioned by using her anchors and winches, but in this maelstrom,
combined with a three-knot tide Carpenter's attempts to reposition his
vessel came to no avail. Tragically, the stormers would now land on a
section of the Mole they found unfamiliar. Instead of landing on the
German battery they would be outside of it separated from their objective
by a defensive strongpoint of impenetrable barbed wire barricades and
enemy machine-gun posts.

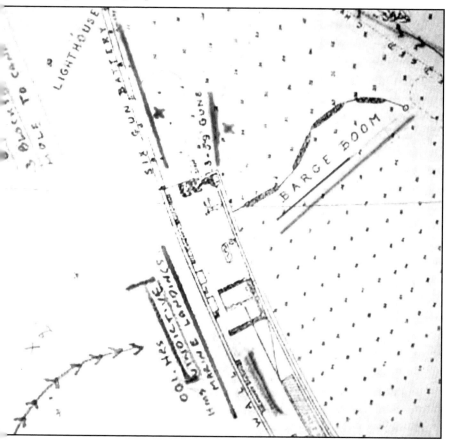

Despite her bulk, *Vindictive* now bobbed up and down like a cork, hampering all Carpenter's efforts to breach the widening gap between her hull and the breakwater. An east-going tide was surging past and in the restricted space between *Vindictive*'s hull and the sheer wall, it became a violent tidal race. The breach between the mother ship and the Mole became insurmountable; despite Carpenter juggling his propellers and rudders it became impossible to close the gap. Huge hooks should have grasped the parapet, but it proved impossible to hook the specially designed Mole grapnels in place.

The Wallasey ferries *Iris* and *Daffodil* had a considerable distance to

The *Daffodil* shown post-raid with her seamen demolition party and their covering party of twenty two men from 4/RMLI.

cover; they cut a corner off their intended route and raced at full steam to the Mole. The *Vindictive* drew most of the fire but *Daffodil* had taken at least one hit. Her commander, Lieutenant Harold G. Campbell, was struck in the eye by a shell splinter that for the time deprived him of the sight in one eye. Instead of landing her raiders, the ferry shoved *Vindictive* against the Mole. Normally *Daffodil*'s boilers developed eighty pounds of pressure per inch; Artificer Engineer Sutton, in charge of them, maintained double the working pressure for the duration of the boat's arduous task. Without this assistance, the storming parties would have been unable to disembark or rejoin the ship. Some of the raiders on board *Daffodil* clambered over her bow onto *Vindictive*'s deck, to disembark over her gangways. Due to the ferry's sheltered position, her casualties during the action were small; one man was killed and a further eight were wounded. A couple of minutes later *Iris* arrived; she steamed past to take up position one hundred yards (30 metres) further along the Mole.

As the gap reduced, the surviving storming parties clambered over the mass of wounded and dead in readiness to scramble ashore. Numbers 10 and 11 Platoons from C [Plymouth] Company had suffered badly. At the foot of the gangway was a prostrate Lieutenant Walker; a shell had carried his left arm away and in the darkness he was mistaken for dead and

trampled on, until he was noticed. As he was carried away to the dressing station, he is reputed to have cried 'Good luck boys, good luck!' The majority of the landing brows were splintered wrecks; they were either smashed against the sea wall or wrecked by gunfire. The two forward brows reached the wall and although they crashed up and down like seesaws due to the ship's movement, the men scurried up them. One survivor remarked 'In the anxiety to keep my balance on the seesaw of the gangway I forgot about the rain of lead, I really felt comfortable when I put my feet on concrete.' Lieutenant Commander B.F. Adams led the naval storming parties, the marines, led by Captain and Adjutant A.R. Chater, closely followed them.

Seaman Wainwright graphically described the landing.

After what seemed an eternity, the anchor rattled down and the all fast signal was given. Out of sixteen gangways only two remained, but these were already in position and up into the night went one huge yell, all the pent up feeling of the years of war and hatred and the lust for killing,

Lieutenant H. T. C. Walker, RN.
He lost an arm on the Mole.

69

and the seamen's storming party landed, followed by the Royal Marines.

To many that yell was their last earthly sound, as the Germans kept up a concentrated machine-gun fire on the gangways, and the dead were piled up three or four deep, but the remnants of the platoon staggered through, reorganised, and carried on as though still in the peaceful heart of Kent.

To see these men, the cream of England, laughing, cheering, and swearing rushing into what seemed certain death, was not inspiring; it was heartbreaking to think that in these enlightened days the youth of the country was being butchered in the cause of civilisation, and Saint Peter must have wiped his eye as he greeted most of them home.

Iris was in difficulty; dwarfed by the towering Mole she struggled to secure herself alongside to disembark her marauders. Stranded on board were A [Chatham] Company Royal Marines and D Company naval storming party. After several attempts to secure these anchors failed, Lieutenant Claude E. K. Hawkings, one of the storming parties' officers, ordered some men to hold up a scaling ladder. Due to the yawing of the ferry, it was impossible to prop the ladder against the sea wall. Undaunted Hawkings ran up the ladder and leapt onto the parapet, just as the ladder was smashed to matchwood. Astride the parapet, he attempted to secure the grapnel while under enemy attack. He valiantly attempted to drive them off with his revolver but died in the process.

Lieutenant Commander George N. Bradford, an excellent all round sportsman and Welterweight Boxing champion of the Royal Navy, was in command of the *Iris* storming parties. Although not responsible for mooring the ferry, he gallantly climbed up the ferry's derrick from which hung the parapet anchor. The ship was still rolling and pitching about but Bradford bided his time before leaping across the gap, and placed the anchor in position. He immediately drew the attention of the machine-gunners; his bullet-riddled body toppled into the watery void between the ferry and Mole. Bradford was born on St. George's Day 1887; fate decreed the County Durham man died on his

Lieutenant Claude E. K. Hawkings, RN. Killed while attempting to secure *Iris*.

thirty-first birthday. Gallant attempts to recover his body failed; Petty Officer M.D. Hallihan died in the process. Bradford received a posthumous VC. Despite his gallantry Bradford had died in vain for the anchor was either shot away or slipped; *Iris* now slewed out from the Mole. Lieutenant Commander Gibbs now decided to steam to the stern of *Vindictive* and discharge his men across her decks.

On *Vindictive,* two other landing brows were brought back into service and a steady stream of men exhibiting tremendous gallantry were now reaching the Mole. These men were encouraged by the continuous covering fire emitting from *Vindictive*'s fighting top. Shrapnel had severed the fuel pipes of Brock's flamethrowers; a valuable piece of defensive hardware was now useless. Within the bullet-riddled fighting top Lieutenant Charles N.B. Rigby of the RMA with his eight fellow marines maintained a continuous fire with pompom and Lewis guns, changing swiftly from one target to another. Their primary targets were the battery at the end of the Mole and the lighter battery on the Mole extension. For good measure they also engaged a *Torpedoboat V69* berthed along the inner wall; the raiders also attacked this with grenades.

The fighting top was drawing increased fire until a tremendous crash announced a direct hit on the position, followed by a cessation of covering fire. The fighting top was a shambles; except for three wounded gunners the others were dead. Sergeant Finch RMA extricated himself from the wreckage, and though severely wounded in the arm examined the remaining weapon, found it serviceable and put it to action. He continued to fire using his remaining arm until a second shell smashed the top and wounded him a second time. Despite being wounded, Gunner Sutton fired the remainder of the ammunition when Finch could no longer continue. Eventually the fighting top was destroyed; Finch survived to receive a well-earned Victoria Cross.

Sergeant Norman Augustus Finch VC.

Lieutenant Commander Sir Edward Hilton Young [Lord Kennet] RNVR:

> *I went back on board to rejoin the guns' crews at the prescribed meeting place in the starboard battery. Whilst making my way thither across the dark and littered deck, I stumbled over somebody at the foot of one of the wooden ramps that led to the landing deck. As well as I could see in the dark there was a platoon still waiting there crouched on the deck. A marine officer looked down from the*

71

landing platform. "*Aren't these folks going over?*" *I asked.* "*Those are all gone,*" *he said.*

The mid-ship 7.5 inch howitzer was also damaged by shellfire and some of its crew were killed. The remaining men frantically worked through a hail of splinters to repair the weapon. Some time later, this piece joined in with the eleven inch howitzer positioned on the quarterdeck, which remained in use throughout the action.

The leading block ships were due to round the Mole twenty-five minutes after *Vindictive* arrived. The diversionary tactics were now in full swing, any members of the storming parties familiar with the Charge of the Light Brigade now found themselves in a very similar position. Although they were not in the valley of death, they were in a restricted killing field against obstacles they could not outflank but were required to advance head on towards the enemy. This assault was further restricted for once onto the parapet they had to negotiate the approximately seven foot (2.3m) wide walkway and while doing so were subject to attack from the Mole garrison. At intervals, stairs connected the parapet with the quayside some sixteen feet (4.9m) below. The maximum width of the battle zone was 240 feet (74m), into which the enemy poured all available firepower later augmented with gas shells.

The Mole action

The first troops to drop onto the Mole were the survivors of A and B Companies from the naval storming party, led by Lieutenant Commander Bryan F. Adams and Lieutenant G.B.T. Chamberlain respectively. Both companies had suffered severely before landing, especially B Company. Adams took command after the senior officer of the naval parties, Commander Harrison, was rendered unconscious by a shell splinter. After completing his duties in the after flamethrower hut the inventor, Wing Commander Brock, went ashore. Although technically not one of the raiders, he had convinced Keyes that he alone was the best man to investigate a secret German sound range finding system mounted on the Mole. It was a foolhardy decision to allow such a valuable asset as this young genius to participate in the landing, for his talents lay elsewhere.

Adams led a small group along the narrow parapet; no easy task for the entire Mole was under constant shell and small-arms fire. As they progressed seaward, they found an observation post; they hurled a bomb in before bursting in only to find it was unoccupied. Some accounts state Brock entered the hut, which was an observation or control station having a range finder behind and above it. From this point Brock's death becomes unclear, and open to speculation.

A member of the Naval storming party in a *Morning Post* interview

Storming the Mole. Drawn in 1921 by Charles de Larcey.

published on 27 April 1918 gave the following account of Brock's end.

> *We were one of the earliest crowds to go over, and Commander Brock went ahead. It was a fearful job getting over the brow, but the Commander dropped down on the Mole, a distance of fifteen feet. 'Come on, you boys,' he shouted and one by one we followed him. There were Huns near us in a nest surrounded by barbed wire, but we stormed that and reached one of the guns on the Mole. Commander Brock, single-handed, attacked the gun's crew, and we captured the gun and put it out of action. Then we went further along the Mole, and in the light of the star shells, I saw the officer fighting the crew of another gun. The last time I saw him he was removing one of the locks of the gun. He shouted to us to go on, and said that he was coming too, but I never saw him again. A Marine told me that just before we went back to the ship he saw Commander Brock wounded and being held up against the side of the Mole by two Marines, who refused to leave him.*

Close to the observation position, an iron ladder descended to the quay; three of Adams' men climbed down, before eliminating several enemy as they attempted to reach the harbour side of the Mole. A machine gun located 100 yards (30 metres) westward, in the trench system of the Mole, maintained a continual fire upon the parapet. This defensive position separated the raiders from their objective; the seaward battery.

By necessity the strongpoint had to be tackled, the seamen bombed the trench but incurred many casualties from the machine-gun fire, and the German warships berthed on the opposite side of the Mole breakwater. Commander Harrison regained consciousness and, despite his broken

74

jaw, he rejoined his men on the parapet. On receiving Adams' report, he sent him for reinforcements. Major Weller, commanding Royal Marines, on receiving Adams' report, despatched Lieutenant G. Underhill with reinforcements for Harrison. Due to the level of casualties, the raiders were hampered by a lack of men compounded by the marooning of D Company still on board *Iris*. While the reinforcements mustered, Adams returned to the observation station where he learned of Harrison's death. Commander Harrison had gathered his handful of men, then led a charge along the exposed parapet. By the time they had covered half the distance all but two were dead. Able Seaman Eaves attempted to carry Harrison's body back to *Vindictive*, but was defeated by his own wounds. The courage exemplified by Harrison resulted in a posthumous VC. A severely wounded Able Seamen Eaves was later captured; he received a DSM for his part in the action. The other wounded survivor of Harrison's group continued to fight on; Able Seaman Albert Edward McKenzie of B Company used his Lewis gun to great effect. He had already accounted for several of the enemy as they raced towards a destroyer. Despite being wounded, he continued to fight until a shell fragment shattered the Lewis gun. Severely wounded, he returned to *Vindictive* and he later received the VC after a ballot amongst his peers. Amongst those fighting was Francis Kenelm Donovan, a Royal Engineer serving with the RNAS. He was responsible for manning the flamethrower hut but when this was put out of action he assaulted the Mole brandishing a naval cutlass and

Barbed wire defensive barrier of the Mole fortified zone.

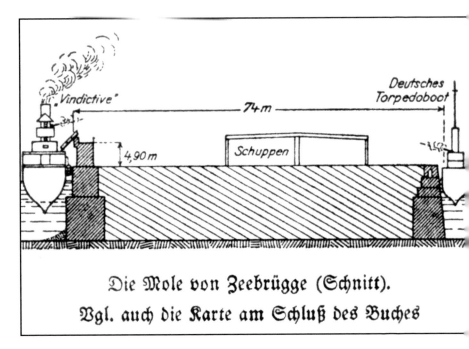

Die Mole von Zeebrügge (Schnitt).
Vgl. auch die Karte am Schluß des Buches

amazingly returned unharmed.

Seaman Wainwright:

Once on the top of the Mole one was assailed by the overwhelming feeling of nakedness and maddening desire to go forward at all costs and stop the hail of death that swept the upper Mole. Sense and reason were replaced by insane fury and the events that followed cannot be remembered coherently; it was a horrible nightmare of sweating and cursing men thirsty for blood, the sickening 'sog' of bayonets and of shots at close quarters.

Three Royal Marine storming parties landed hard on the heels of the naval storming parties. With a ringing cheer and 'Over you go, Royals' the marines headed for the first ledge on the Mole, losing heavily in the process, for the enemy were pulverising the breakwater with their shore batteries. The noise was deafening yet the screams of dying men were still audible. Due to the high casualties incurred by C [Plymouth] Company, their number 5 Platoon under Lieutenant Theodore F. Cooke, and Captain Edward Bamford led the attack in the opposite direction of the seamen. They turned right along the parapet under a move initiated by Captain and adjutant Chater. German riflemen had taken up a position upon the roof of Number 2 Shed some ninety yards distant. From this vantage point they fired into the units disembarking along *Vindictive*'s brows. Despite being wounded, Lieutenant Cooke continued to direct his men, who successfully drove the enemy from the shed roof. Lieutenant C. D. R. Lamplough commanding 9 Platoon and a dozen survivors from 10 Platoon, (thirty-five were already killed or wounded) were next ashore. They descended from the parapet by ropes, a difficult manoeuvre when you have your back to the enemy and are encumbered with equipment. They proceeded to bomb their way to the shoreward end of Number 3 Shed where they established a strongpoint to prevent any expected counter-attack.

Bugler A. W. Forrester had managed to disembark from *Iris*: he once recalled his escape from certain death.

> *As we attacked we sought any available cover; I decided to shelter behind a huge coil of mooring ropes. Instead, I charged past the ropes and when I looked around they were no longer there. A shell had obliterated them.*

The name of Bugler Forrester was entered into the VC ballot.

Other units landed, number 7 Platoon placed heavy scaling ladders in position, before supporting numbers 9 and 10 Platoons. Bamford and Cooke established their position 200 yards (60 metres) from *Vindictive,* greatly assisting the advance along the quay. Lamplough's marines also replied to fire from a moored destroyer, into which they threw several Mills bombs. Major Weller then received the earlier mentioned naval raiding party request for reinforcements. He despatched 12 Platoon and the survivors from 11 Platoon under Lieutenant G. Underhill. The reinforcements reached the look-out station, where they were halted by machine-gun fire. Adams and his men were forty or fifty yards (15 metres) ahead of them; they also could make no progress along the deadly parapet. From the shoreward end, the enemy brought their machine guns to bear on the raiding parties exploring the sheds, hangars and other buildings. Star shells had turned night into day; there were no shadows to conceal the raiders. The enemy awaited reinforcements for a counter-attack but this never occurred due to the intervention of submarine *C3*.

Fourteen-year-old boy bugler Alexander W. Forrester.

Submarine *C3* explodes

To coincide with the landing of the storming parties two submarines would destroy the viaduct. After parting the tow off the Zeebrugge coastline *C1*

CH 13429 Bugler A. W. Forrester RMLI, was wounded in the right shoulder.

developed a mechanical problem; *C3* proceeded on her own towards her objective. The submarine had a hand-picked six-man volunteer crew under the command of Lieutenant Sandford RN. His second in command was Lieutenant Price, RNR; Coxswain Hamer, Chief Engine Room Artificer Roxburgh, Leading Torpedo Operator Cleaver and Stoker Bendall completed the crew.

At midnight, the submarine, running on the surface, entered the shoal waters of Zeebrugge. Her crew were all on deck, and it was a silent and nervy passage. About a mile and a half from the viaduct a star shell illuminated the submarine briefly; she drew fire from the shore. When the wind veered round to the south the smokescreen gradually dispersed. A searchlight beam locked onto *C3*; she then drew considerable small-arms fire from ashore. Unperturbed, Sandford headed straight for the viaduct; at a range of a few hundred yards the firing slackened as the Germans anticipated capturing her. They felt safe in the knowledge the submarine would become ensnared in the viaduct steelwork. Sandford opted against using the gyro steering gear in case of a malfunction; this decision drastically reduced their escape time. At ten knots (11.5mph) *C3* collided into the structure, her hull rose bodily about two feet onto the horizontal girders which penetrated the conning tower.

Sandford immediately started the six-minute clockwork fuse, and then

Crew of the *C3*.

A Belgian postcard captioned – 'The Breach 66 metres long and 20 metres wide, made by the explosion of *C3* laden with 10,000 kilos of dynamite'.

gave the order 'Abandon ship'. They pushed off in the skiff, whose propeller had fouled the exhaust pipe. Her engine was now useless forcing the crew to row for their lives, while under rifle fire from the viaduct.

Coxswain Hamer and Stoker Bendall took the oars until Bendall became unconscious. Cleaver grabbed the oar and carried on until the coxswain was hit. When Bendall received another wound, he and Hamer were moved to the bows to displace the load. The now badly holed skiff caught in the glare of a searchlight drew heavy fire from the viaduct.

Lieutenant Price took the oar, prior to being relieved by Roxburgh when Lieutenant Sandford was hit. At 12.20 a.m., when the skiff was almost 300 yards (90 metres) distant from *C3,* the submarine time bomb ignited in a vast column of flame. A lengthy section of the viaduct disappeared along with 250 of the enemy, the searchlights extinguished and the firing died away.[2] Captain Carpenter during a post raid interview said:

> Suddenly the thing happened for which we had been, semi-consciously, waiting. There was a tremendous roar, and up went a huge tower of flame and debris and bodies into the black sky. My fellows cheered like mad, for they knew what it meant. Sandford had got home beneath the viaduct with his ancient submarine and touched her off. I never saw such a column of flame! It seemed a mile high!

Minutes later a picket boat, commanded by Lieutenant Commander Francis H. Sandford, the elder brother of the submarine commander, rescued the skiff occupants. To quote Captain Carpenter 'Many miracles happened that night, but nothing more miraculous than the escape of these two officers and four men'.

79

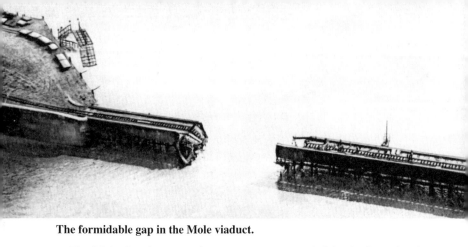

The formidable gap in the Mole viaduct.

The Mole then became a long narrow man-made island where the air reverberated with the cannonading of the guns. Beneath the merciless glare of the star shells, the machine-gun bullets continued to inflict havoc upon the marauders. The depleted attackers faced a dilemma as an attack against the fortified zone may have provided the enemy an opportunity to seize positions alongside *Vindictive* and exploit them with disastrous consequences. On the other hand, the impregnable fortified zone prevented the now severely under strength force from destroying their primary objective. The 5.9 calibre outer guns were capable of destroying the block ships as they rounded the tip of the Mole. Despite having insufficient numbers the raiders determined to press home their attacks; their actions would also distract the artillery crew's attention away from the harbour approach. Had there been a casual bystander on the shell-swept breakwater, he may have noticed the star shells illuminating the tall

A temporary bridge rigged up over the gap.

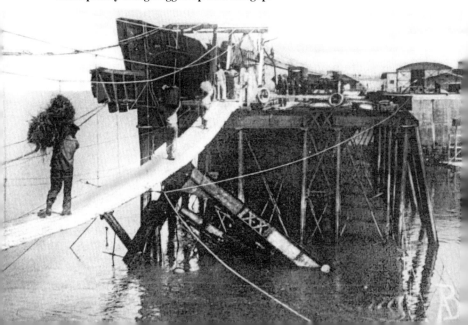

A panoramic view of the Zeebrugge action.

funnels of three block ships stealing in towards the canal entrance.

After securing their secondary objective, Major Weller despatched reinforcements to assist the naval storming party, which had come to a standstill farther seaward. Lieutenant Underhill commanding 12 Platoon, and a handful of 11 Platoon survivors set off towards the Mole extension until temporarily halted by machine-gun fire. Here they noticed a 4.5 inch calibre (90mm) gun still shrouded in its tarpaulin cover, a clear indication some enemy were unable to man their stations. Private James Feeney, Number 7 Platoon Royal Marines, recalled:

> *Captain Bamford then came up and calmly said "Fall in B Company." I fell in with McDowell and Sergeant Brady took charge; there were only 16 there, and Captain Bamford then led us off.*

Ten of the officers were dead; several of the platoons now relied on sergeants for leadership. Captain Bamford in a magnificent example of courage and leadership led numbers 5, 6, and 8 Platoons and whoever he could muster in a renewed diversionary attack on the 4.1 battery.

The Blockships' arrival

After the flotilla separated at point G the block ships reduced speed to allow *Vindictive* and the ferries time to create the diversion. The blockers sailed through the coastal water peppered with artillery bursts; throughout their gun crews stood by ready to repel attack from enemy shipping. They steamed in Indian file led by *Thetis* commanded by Commander Ralph

81

S. Sneyd, in her wake followed *Intrepid*, (Lieutenant Stuart S. Bonham-Carter) and *Iphigenia,* commanded by Lieutenant Edward W. Billyard-Leake brought up the rear. The latter officer replaced Ivan B. Franks who had supervised the early preparations of all the block ships. Two days earlier Franks was hospitalised with appendicitis; before leaving he urged Keyes to pass his command to Billyard-Leake. He was initially hesitant to place such an important role on so young an officer, but a petition from the ship's crew swayed Keyes.

Throughout the mother ship's battering alongside the Mole, a member of the pyrotechnic team fired guiding rockets from a stern window. The rockets were set to burst beyond the lighthouse to guide in the blockers who were also aided by a flotilla of motor launches assigned to navigational and rescue duty.

James Dawbarn Young RNVR was promoted to Lieutenant Commander on 11 July 1917, simultaneously becoming commander of a motor launch division. He received a mention in despatches (MID) 'for services in the 11/12 May 1917 bombardment of Zeebrugge' and the 4/5 June and posthumously for this raid. Young commanded *ML 110*; he volunteered his boat for the extremely hazardous task of preceding the block ships in order to light the harbour and canal entrance with illuminated calcium marker buoys. They laid one buoy but the light was extinguished by a torrent of water from a shell burst. His launch raced in to replace the buoy but in the process, three shells struck *ML 110*, which killed and wounded half of the crew and destroyed the engines. Commander Young, hit in three places was mortally wounded; he resolutely held on to consciousness until he had supervised the transfer of the survivors into the dinghy, before overseeing the sinking of his disabled launch. The gallant officer then collapsed and died.

Lieutenant Commander James Dawburn Young RNVR. Born 2 August 1877, killed at Zeebrugge.

The lighthouse appeared through the smoke just as *ML 558* hailed with directions. *Thetis* raced ahead at full speed; at twenty past midnight she rounded the lighthouse steering for the extremity of the barge boom. Too late the enemy realised the true purpose of the attack; numerous batteries now focussed on the block ships. The storming parties otherwise engaged the Mole's seaward batteries, thereby fulfilling their diversionary role.

The block ships' orders were to enter the canal; if *Thetis* found herself accompanied by both block ships, she was to ram the canal gate. *Intrepid* and *Iphigenia* were to scuttle near the canal entrance, the narrowest section of the channel. Refugee Belgian engineers considered this point most favourable for a rapid build-up of silt around the abandoned cruisers.

Swathed in artificial fog with guns roaring in reply *Thetis* steamed into a tornado of shells from the shore batteries. Her four guns blasted the lighthouse used as a signalling and observation station and sank a barge. She cleared the string of boom barges defending the channel but caught in a strong east-flowing tidal stream she fouled a propeller in the defensive net. Her propellers gathered in the steel net, grinding her engines to a halt. She bumped into a sandbank, edged off then found herself in the main channel again. *Thetis* lay immobile, a sitting duck for the adjacent 6.7 inch guns of the *Friedrichsort* battery. There she lay 300 yards (90 metres) from the canal entrance repeatedly shelled and on fire; and settling lower in the water. The stricken vessel then fired a green signal rocket signalling her consorts to pass to starboard. *Intrepid* then *Iphigenia* steamed past; Captain Sneyd ordered the smoke apparatus to be turned on prior to abandoning ship. Despite both engines being disabled and the 'clear the engine room' order given, Engineering Lieutenant Commander Ronald C. Boddie and Frank Marsden returned to the engine where they succeeded in getting the engine to drive forward; Boddie received a DSO, Marsden was also decorated.

The ship was now scraping her bottom on the seabed but made sufficient headway to scuttle across the dredged channel. The petty officer responsible for the forward firing keys had been killed; it proved impossible to find them in the fumes from the bursting shells and smokescreen. A duplicate firing mechanism at the stern was employed; after ordering the crew on deck Sneyd blew the bottom out of *Thetis*. In a few moments she sank, her upper deck was now just under the surface.

The wreck of HMS *Thetis*.

The block ship was still under fire; two out of her three escape boats were wrecked by shellfire. The crew took to the only remaining, but badly holed, boat and then pulled away from the wreck. Acting Lieutenant Belben [awarded a DSO] took command of the overcrowded, badly waterlogged boat, keeping her afloat until they were rescued. Many of the smaller vessels played a major contribution throughout the entire operation. Time after time, the flimsy craft braved the storm of steel to fulfil their assigned orders. The DSO citation for Lieutenant Hugh A. L. Littleton RNVR records how he handled *ML 526* in a magnificent manner. Under heavy machine-gun fire at close range, he embarked over sixty officers and men from *Thetis*. It was solely through his courage and daring that his boat succeeded in making good her escape with the survivors of *Thetis*. Her losses were five killed and five wounded, the latter including Sneyd and his second in command, both gassed.

Intrepid, smoking like a volcano, directed by *Thetis* aground on her port hand, now swept through the vast opening created by her predecessor. On approaching the Mole, she came under heavy shrapnel fire; she replied with all guns blazing. During the final run to the canal she was unmolested by gunfire, which was concentrated on *Vindictive* and *Thetis*. After locating the entrance piers, the cruiser entered the canal to a point just inland of the coastline. Ahead lay the Bruges canal lock gate that *Thetis* intended to destroy; we can only conjecture whether *Intrepid* should have rammed the gate, effectively putting the cork in the bottle. An excellent opportunity went begging. Perhaps it was no time for initiative but adhering to every letter of his orders (to sink his vessel across the channel), Lieutenant Bonham-Carter went full ahead with the starboard engine and full speed astern with the port helm hard a starboard. Once in position he ordered the crew to the lifeboats. The reader may recall the protestations of her surplus crew to remain on board; instead of a crew of fifty-four, she had eighty-seven on board. As the alarm bell rang, the ship began to drift astern, aided by *Iphigenia* slamming into her port bow. Bonham-Carter hurriedly flicked the switches in the chart room; four dull bumps announced the detonation of the mines in the warship's bowels. Engineering Sub-Lieutenant Meikle and three engine room ratings emerged from the engine room unaffected by the explosions. Now in her death throes, *Intrepid* began to settle; her engines still made sufficient headway to hold her in position into the sandbank until she bedded down on the bottom. On her deck, Leading Seaman Davis had remained, vainly awaiting the order to destroy his gun. The order never came; Davis remained at his post until the ship sank under him and then swam to a boat.

One badly overloaded cutter pulled out to sea; the occupants were rescued by *ML 526*, which had already saved the crew of *Thetis*. Another cutter rowed out beyond the Mole until the destroyer *Whirlwind* rescued them. Lieutenant Bonham-Carter, Lieutenant Cory Wright, his second in command, Sub Lieutenant Babb, the navigator, and four petty officers were the last to leave the stricken *Intrepid*. They launched a flimsy Carley raft and proceeded to paddle it to safety, however the Germans had a machine gun on shore within close range, intent on sinking the raft. A lifebuoy light inadvertently left on the raft automatically lit up on contact with water. This small beacon revealed their movement; all attempts to extinguish the light initially failed. They even sat on it but could not obscure or destroy it for some time. The machine-gun bullets were cutting up the water all around them and it was only due to the choppy sea and the swathes of artificial smoke emitting from their abandoned ship that none of the party died. *ML 282,* commanded by Lieutenant Percy Dean, RNVR, had crept up the canal beneath the stern of *Iphigenia*, which drew considerable fire. The launch rescued the Carley float occupants who managed to clamber aboard safely. However, Bonham-Carter was now in the water unseen; as the motor launch engines roared into life he managed to grab a trailing rope. For some time he bounced along on the end of the rope buffeted by the waves. Unable to hold on any longer the rope slid from his grasp; by good fortune he was noticed floundering in the water, then rescued by the launch. Another officer had jumped ashore and raced for all he was worth along the bank to the launch. During his dash for freedom, a machine-gun bullet stung him; he now leapt for the motor launch. Appearing out of the dark onto the pitching launch a

The wreck of *Iphegenia* and *Intrepid*.

startled crewmember wasted no time in determining the allegiance of the late arrival who was promptly attacked with a hammer. All bar one of *Intrepid*'s crew survived the ordeal, chiefly due to the heroism of *ML 282*. Stoker Petty Officer Harold L. Pallister was killed by machine-gun fire while in the motor launch.

The third block ship, *Iphigenia,* commanded by Lieutenant Edward W. Billyard-Leake, followed a few minutes behind *Intrepid*. She passed through waters disturbed by the incessant geysers thrown up by off target shells. Suddenly the beam from a pair of shore based searchlights locked on *Iphigenia*, who immediately attracted heavy shrapnel fire. As she rounded the lighthouse, a star shell exploded briefly showing *Intrepid* steaming towards the canal. The wreck of *Thetis* with her green light glowing through the choking acrid smoke guided Billyard-Leake clear of the sandbank. As she passed *Thetis,* two shots possibly intended for her slammed into the starboard side of *Iphigenia.* One shell severed the siren steam pipe shrouding the forecastle in steam. Her commander, blinded by the billowing smoke streaming from *Iphigenia*, nearly missed the canal entrance. She blindly sailed on through the impenetrable fog, until the west pier suddenly loomed up.

Her commander ordered 'full speed astern'; while still making headway she rammed a dredger with a barge alongside it, which lay at the western arm of the canal. She got clear though and entered the canal pushing the barge before her.

Noticing a gap between *Intrepid*'s bow and the eastern bank of the canal, *Iphigenia* headed to close it, in the process colliding with the bow

The channel blocked to all major shipping.

At 11 a.m. on 23 April 1918, a German aviator took this photograph of
Intrepid. **She is still emitting steam from the forecastle.**

of *Intrepid*. Billyard-Leake rang the 'abandon ship' alarm, but as his vessel had not completely blocked the channel, he telegraphed to the engine room to go astern. As soon as his ship cleared, he despatched First Lieutenant Philip E. Vaux to the engine room with an order to go ahead. When the ship had headway, he put the port engine astern, the starboard ahead, and his helm hard a starboard, slewing the vessel diagonally across the channel and grounded on the eastern bank. Engineering Mate Sydney West returned to the engine room to ensure *Iphigenia* maintained forward momentum. Throughout, this ship was under machine-gun fire from the shore. After prolonged manoeuvring a supremely confident Lieutenant E.W. Billyard-Leake considered he could not improve on *Iphigenia*'s position astern of *Intrepid*. He flicked the switches for destroying the cruiser; they left her with engines going to hold her in position until she bedded down on the bottom. Next day a British admiralty statement reported 'According to reports from air observation, the two ships, with their holds full of concrete, are lying across the canal in a V position; and the work they set out to do has been accomplished. The canal is effectively blocked'.

The scuttling of *Iphigenia* came as a relief to the rescue motor launch waiting close to her stern. Already half filled with some of *Intrepid*'s crew she was an equally attractive target to the machine-gunner. The launch

Mission accomplished. The western side of the blocked channel.

commander later remarked 'It seemed that the damned fellow was never going to stop juggling with his engines'.

As her crew abandoned ship, the spare engine room ratings emerged; contrary to orders they had also remained on board beyond position G. It was a sign of the determination of the crews to engage the enemy that a warship should have so many stowaways; they now added to the difficulties of evacuation. As one of the ship's boats was severely damaged, the full complement crammed into one cutter. Lieutenant Dean had steamed *ML 282* straight into the canal and stopped between the two sunken block ships. She came under constant and deadly fire from machine and heavy guns at point blank range, yet was undeterred from the rescue work. When *ML 282* was sighted across the bow of *Iphigenia,* the cutter pulled up to her, and most of the crew climbed on board. The remainder (one dead), turned the cutter and then gained the dubious safety of the launch.

The cutter herself was secured to the launch bows as, having just picked up the raft party from *Intrepid*, she had continued heading up the canal. The launch now went full astern and backed out of the canal, stern first, with the cutter in tow. No less than 101 survivors from the block ships were crammed on board the launch. Under usual circumstances such craft are capable of carrying forty to fifty passengers at a squeeze. Now dangerously low in the water and considerably top heavy due to her 101 wounded and tired men, Lieutenant Dean turned his boat round as soon

88

as he was clear of the canal.

It proved an inopportune time for a steering gear fault; undeterred he steered the boat by working the engines at unequal speeds. While juggling his twin engines he took a brave gamble by passing as close to the Mole as he considered prudent. His very proximity to the batteries ensured their barrels could not depress sufficiently to target his craft. Mercifully, the overloaded launch passed unnoticed by the Mole defenders, whose small-arms fire or stick grenades could not have failed to hit their target.

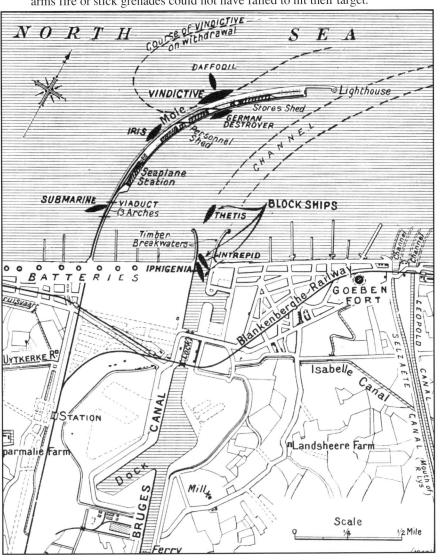

After passing the breakwater, the overladen launch steered northwestward. Keyes' *Warwick*, with its enormous flag, bore towards them; they all leapt to their feet cheering their rescuer wildly, while almost capsizing the launch.

The continuous heavy machine-gun fire caused many casualties. The crew of *ML 282* paid a heavy price, one officer and two men (out of 4) laid down their lives in this splendid achievement and Second Officer J. Wright was dangerously wounded. The gallantry of the launch crew successfully rescued over 100 men from the expected 'suicide mission'. Few of the block ship crews expected to return home; without the efforts of *ML 282* those rescued would inevitably have faced internment. In recognition of their gallantry, Lieutenant Percy Thompson Dean RNVR received the Victoria Cross.

Eleven torpedo boat destroyers were involved in the inshore operations. Keyes had a roving commission on board *Warwick*, directing operations from the vicinity of the lighthouse. The destroyers *North Star*, Lieutenant Commander K.C. Helyar, and *Phoebe,* commanded by Lieutenant Commander H.E. Gore-Langton, guarded the storming vessels alongside the Mole. Constantly under fire from the shore batteries, they operated beneath smokescreens. Emerging from the suffocating smoke *North Star* found herself within the harbour to eastward of the Mole. As the block ships dashed for the canal, *North Star* launched torpedoes at a destroyer inside the harbour. As she steered clear of the harbour entrance, a salvo of shells fired at point blank range disabled her completely. Her main steam joint fractured and the harsh noise of escaping steam was deafening. Her consort *Phoebe,* carrying *C3*'s crew transferred from the steam pinnace, now came to her aid. Under cover of a smokescreen attempts were made to take the battered wreck in tow; gunfire frustrated all attempts, wires were broken by shells as soon as they made fast.

V. Mogg, a telegraphist on *Phoebe* wrote:

Both destroyers were now clear of the covering smoke and the enemy, seeing us thus exposed, fired with redoubled energy. The North Star, *being nearer to the shore, suffered heavy damage, shells seemed to strike her continuously.*

Phoebe attempted to push *North Star* clear of the batteries, but this proved impossible. After forty-five minutes of salvage attempts Helyar reluctantly ordered 'Abandon ship'.

Men began to scramble across the gap between the two ships; some slipped and fell between, some were able to get back, but others had a difficult job as the water was covered with an oily slime. Boats were lowered but sank as soon as they touched the water,

A post-raid photograph showing part of the company of *Phoebe*. Vernon Mogg is immediately above the second man from the right in the front row.

their hulls being full of holes from small shell fragments. Ropes were thrown over the side and some managed to get back by that method, but it was a difficult job in the dark.　Telegraphist V. Mogg

Ninety-nine officers and men from a complement of about one hundred and twenty clambered on *Phoebe*. Lieutenant Commander Gore-Langton now had his own ship's survival plus two ships' companies on board to consider.

I made my way to the after canopy. Lying there on an improvised stretcher was a badly wounded member of the North Star*'s crew. He was covered in blankets; his was a hopeless case. We could see his life's blood trickling from under the blankets and over the ship's side and he passed away before Dover.*　　　　　　V. Mogg

At 2.30 a.m. *Phoebe* steamed away from Zeebrugge, heading for safety. The shore batteries pulverised *North Star* until she slid beneath the waves at a position north-east of the lighthouse. Five of her crew listed in the records as killed actually became prisoners of war.[3]

Following the destruction of the viaduct and the sighting of block ships heading for the canal, *Vindictive*'s role was almost over. The *Daffodil* was still gamely pressing the battered cruiser to the Mole. Carpenter was acutely aware that should the ferry be disabled *Vindictive* would veer away from the Mole, thereby stranding the raiding parties. The upper works of the cruiser were perforated and in tatters, any guns capable of engaging the Mole were out of action. The only possible advantage gained by remaining lay in the destruction of any structures or defences. Due to the conditions ashore, the demolition work had not been carried out. The raiders were in such close proximity to each other the detonation

91

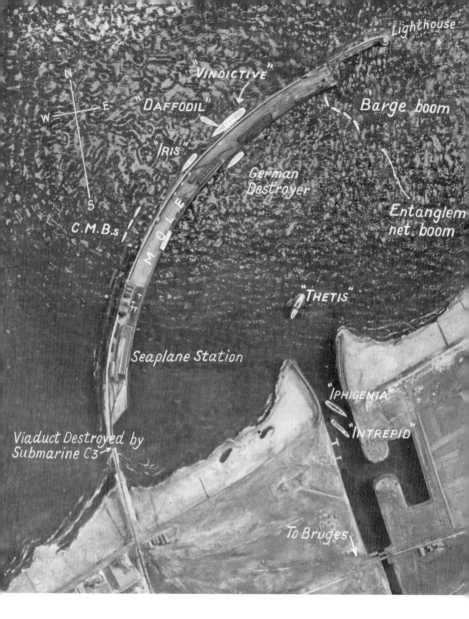

of the amatol charges would have endangered their own side. Furthermore the destruction exacted on the Mole by the coastal batteries appeared sufficient. Captain Carpenter made the wise decision to curtail the operation ahead of schedule.

Iris had abandoned all attempts to secure to the Mole. Her commander, Valentine Gibbs, ordered the cable to be slipped and then steamed round the stern of *Daffodil* and came abreast of *Vindictive*. The crew of the mother ship were so preoccupied with events on the Mole, they at first failed to notice *Iris*. A precious forty minutes had passed before *Iris* moored to the cruiser; her marines began to jump into the *Vindictive*. It was now 12.55 a.m.; too much time had elapsed so those on *Iris* were ordered to remain on board. *Iris* was to sail immediately to the pre-arranged rendezvous point, where she would, hopefully, unite with her consorts.

It was a bitter blow to A Company on board *Iris* for they had come within a grenade's throw of the enemy. Lieutenant Sir Edward Hilton Young [wounded at the start of the action, he later had his arm amputated] on board *Vindictive* watched the ferry depart:

The sirens bellowed, we cast off Iris*'s hawser, and backing away from our side she steamed out to sea on a course that took her right across the front of the Mole batteries at four or five hundred yards distance. I watched with a sinking heart, knowing how we had suffered on the way in. She had not gone five hundred yards before the batteries began to crash and bang. It was a terrible thing to watch. At that short range, the light fabric of the little ship was hulled* [sic] *through and through, flames and smoke spurting from her far side as the shells struck her.*

Iris juddered from stem to stern as the explosions ripped through her. In swift succession, a series of six-inch shells found the Wallasey boat. Two shells of twelve-inch diameter devastated her, the conning house at the extremity of the port wing was wrecked, and the other burst on the main deck, fanning flames along her wooden decks. The first heavy shell had mortally wounded Commander Valentine Gibbs; also Major Eagles, the navigating officer, lay seriously wounded. Out of control, the ferry lurched to starboard throwing her at the mercy of more shore batteries.

From down below Lieutenant Oscar Henderson led a volunteer fire party onto the upper deck to quench the fire amongst the ammunition ready for the landing. Sharp orders were issued; he then raced up to the destroyed wheelhouse, amid scenes of utter carnage, he took command of the vessel.

A single big shell plunged through the upper deck and burst below at a point where fifty-six marines were waiting the order to go to the gangways [order earlier cancelled]. *Forty-nine were killed and the remaining seven wounded. Another shell in the wardroom, which was serving as a sick bay, killed four officers and twenty-six men. Her total casualties were eight officers and sixty-nine men killed and three officers and 102 men wounded.*
Wallasey News, 27 April 1918.

Iris was still in extreme danger; only seconds had passed since the first

93

The main deck position on *Iris*, where the chief loss of life took place.

shells struck home, and she remained a target no gunner could resist. The navigating officer, George Spencer, lay seriously wounded and barely conscious, yet had sufficient wits about him to plot a course for Petty Officer David P. Smith. As Smith spun the ship's wheel away from land, a barrage of 3.5 and 4 inch shells straddled *Iris*; shells burst through her upper works. Amazingly, the ferry survived; *ML 558* had seen the plight of *Iris* and now came racing to her aid. Disregarding the danger, Lieutenant Commander Chapell DSC lay a protective smokescreen around *Iris*. The shore batteries continued to pump shells blindly into the retreating black cloud; *ML 558* was herself damaged by shellfire.

An Australian Acting Artificer Engineer, William Henry Edgar, accompanied by Engine Room Artificer third class Stanley G.

Private Aldridge in his Wallasey police uniform, pre RMLI.

94

Odam, ventured onto the shrapnel-swept deck to carry out repairs to the smoke apparatus. As *ML 558* braced herself for another run, *Iris* belched out Brock's acrid smoke and disappeared in her own smokescreen. Several parting shots hit the tortured ferry whose double hull could be the only reason as to why she remained afloat.

Iris was now a floating hearse; her decks strewn with the dead whose numbers steadily increased. Surgeon Frank Pearce Pocock RAMC was the sole survivor of the sick bay staff, now responsible for over 100 wounded men. He would spend over thirteen hours at his makeshift operating table. Throughout he worked under candle and torch light, for *Iris*'s dynamo no longer worked.

Among the severely wounded was twenty-nine-year-old Private Richard Aldridge; a six-foot three tall marine, a former Wallasey police officer and a winner of the police cross-river Mersey swimming race. He was a married man who originally intended joining the Guards; instead, he joined the RMLI circa 1915. As a resident of Poulton, Wallasey, in halcyon times he would have sailed many times on board the ferries. At Zeebrugge he was peppered with shrapnel and later died at Chatham.

In the blackened wheel house Valentine Gibbs edged closer to death; with both legs blown off he remained at his post, never once enquiring about his wounds. Gibbs' claim to fame lay in winning the Cresta Run at St. Moritz; perhaps this memory comforted him as he lay in agony, as no morphia was available. Wounded at 1.10 a.m., through sheer determination he survived until 9.30. George Spencer's pulse beat weaker; alongside him Petty Officer Smith remained at his post, steering with one hand while lighting the compass with a torch held in the other. He was joined by the wounded Signalman Bryant; originally taken below to the surgeon, he had insisted on returning to the bridge. Bryant, the only surviving signaller, lay propped against a bulkhead receiving and sending signals. He lapsed in and out of consciousness due to the excruciating pain from two mangled legs.

As *Iris* limped home, Lieutenant Henderson returned to take charge of the fire party; only Able Seaman Blake had survived. Ferdinand Blake originally belonged to the seaman storming party; throughout the heavy shrapnel fire he had doggedly extinguished fires under the bridge with sand. He assisted Henderson in throwing

Commander Valentine F. Gibbs, RN who died on board *Iris*.

A post-raid image of *Vindictive*, showing the wrecked brows and superstructure.

overboard live Stokes and Mills bombs, which were lying in the burning debris on the deck. Bryant returned with Henderson to the bridge; despite his badly burned hands. Blake took over the wheel, remaining there for six hours.

With her forward compartments flooded and her condenser leaking, Artificer Engineer W.H. Edgar coaxed over eight knots from the Mersey-built engines. Inside an engine room shrouded in poisonous smoke fumes, since *Iris*'s brush with death he remained at his post. *Iris* met up with escort ships that were unable to tow her due to the forward flooding. She limped into Dover at 2.45 p.m. to a tumultuous welcome; Edgar had then been at his post for over thirteen hours without a break.

Twenty minutes before the general retirement signal *Vindictive* was to sweep the Mole with her searchlight. When her steam whistle blasted out the Morse signal K for Keyes, the raiders were to re-embark. Often criticised as over elaborate, a specific signal was necessary as steam ships often announced their arrival and departure by whistle blasts. One such whistle may inadvertently have caused a premature withdrawal.

Vindictive had taken such terrible punishment that neither her searchlights or siren worked; instead, *Daffodil* signalled the retirement. At 12.50 a.m., a low noise emitted gradually rising up the scale to an ear-piercing shriek of intermittent blasts. Simultaneously crates of fused Stoke mortar bombs were set on fire by a shell. As all convenient fire fighting equipment had been shot away Chief Quartermaster Petty Officer E. G. Youlton improvised. After shouting to the others to take cover, he pulled out the burning boxes and stamped on them to extinguish the flames. Shortly after the flames burst out again; he repeated his heroic efforts. Perplexed by the strange signal Captain Chater returned on board to confirm the recall. He now beckoned the marines back to *Vindictive*; on seeing his desperate waving Captain Bamford called off the marines' seaward attack. As they withdrew, Corporal Kingshott and Private A.G. Clarke reported the battery at the end of the Mole was out of action. This may have been due to the raiders' fire, for the block ships passed the

HMS *Vindictive* on her return from Zeebrugge, showing the bridge, fighting top and flame thrower hut on the right. Below this hut is a battery of Stokes mortars. A large shell passed through the hole to the right of the man in the white uniform.

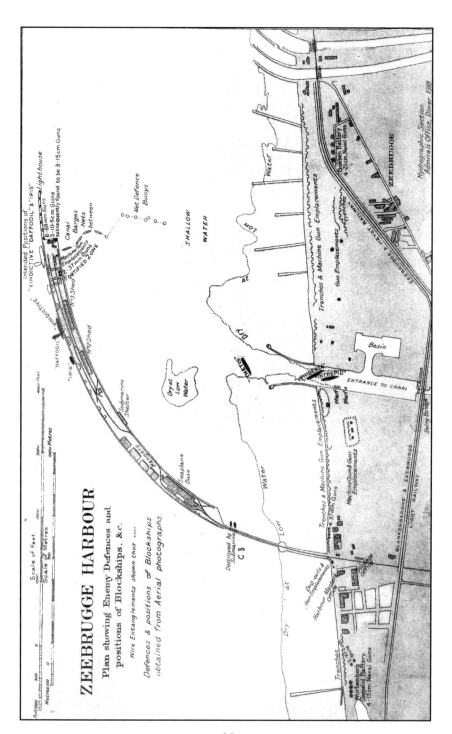

ZEEBRUGGE HARBOUR

Plan showing Enemy Defences and positions of Blockships, &c.

Wire Entanglements shown thus ....

Defences & positions of Blockships obtained from Aerial photographs.

Scale of Feet
Scale of Metres

Intended Positions of "VINDICTIVE" "DAFFODIL" & "IRIS"

6·88mm Guns
3·10·5cm Guns
Subsequently found to be 3·15·cm Guns
Net Defence Buoys
Canal Barges Nets between
2·37mm Guns
FORTIFIED ZONE
Machine Gun Emplacements

Lighthouse
VINDICTIVE
DAFFODIL
"IRIS"
N'3 Shed
N'2 Shed
Submarine Shelter
SEAPLANE
Seaplane Base
Destroyed by Submarines
C 3
Dug outs & Gun Emplacements
Harbour Master office
Trenches
Yürtzemberg (Tappers) Battery 4·15cm Naval Guns

SHALLOW WATER
Dry at Low Water

Water
Low at
KJ D
MOT at
Water
Low at Dry

ZEEBRUGGE
Mole Battery 4·21cm Naval Guns
AVIATION TERRAIN TERRAIN
Trenches & Machine Gun Emplacements
Gun Emplacements
Basin
INTREPID
THETIS
IPHIGENIA
Wharf
ENTRANCE TO CANAL
Wharf
Trenches & Machine Gun Emplacements
4·37mm Guns
Machine Gun & Gun Emplacement
BLANKENBERGHE & ZEEBRUGGE LIGHT RAILWAY
Swing Bridge
Sluices

Hydrographic Section, Admiral's Office, Dover. 1918.

battery unscathed.

Lieutenant Lamplough, commanding 9 Platoon, held the position closest to the breach; they now covered the retirement. The attacking force fell back in good order, running the gauntlet of German weaponry, often carrying on their backs wounded comrades. They had no option other than climbing the scaling ladder, gambling with death on the parapet, or using a creaking brow. The enemy now concentrated their fire on the retiring raiders' point of exit. Captain Chater RMLI remained by the scaling ladders, urging exhausted raiders for one more surge of energy. Encumbered with their weaponry and frequently burdened with wounded, the ladder proved a severe test of stamina and determination. Captain C. P. Tuckey remained at the foot of the only remaining gangway, shepherding his flock up the gangways; he died whilst doing so. While carrying a wounded man back to the ladders Lieutenant Cooke received another severe head wound; his attendant, Private Press, the battalion runner, stayed with the unconscious officer and, despite his own wounds, managed to carry him on board.

Captain Palmer of C Company (Plymouth) conducted his company retirement with men from number 9 and 10 Platoons. His rear guard comprised two sergeants, a corporal and ten privates, including two wounded and failed to reach *Vindictive* before she sailed.

Sergeant Harry Price of 10 Platoon explained why he spent the remainder of the war in a prison camp:

The signal to retire should have been a succession of short blasts, instead the other ship made a succession of long and short blasts.
We took it however for the signal to retire and commenced doing so when the order was passed that it was not the retire signal and we were ordered back to our posts. We obeyed the order and very shortly afterwards we had the terrible ordeal of seeing our only means of escape slowly move away.

A shell burst outside the conning tower; hot metal shards gouged into the legs of Lieutenant Commander Rosoman, shattered the arm of Petty Officer Youlton and Carpenter received a wound to the shoulder. Fifteen minutes after the recall signal Captain Carpenter was informed men had ceased boarding his vessel. As a safeguard, Carpenter waited until 1.10 a.m. before ordering *Daffodil* to tow *Vindictive* clear of the Mole. The tow snapped almost immediately but her bow was

Later Lord Kennet, former Minister of Health. Known at Zeebrugge as Lieutenant Edward Hilton Young M.P. RNVR.

99

sufficiently clear to make headway. Hidden in a cloud of choking smoke *Vindictive* steered for home.

I then remembered what I had seen when the Iris *passed the batteries, and I thought "In two minutes that will be happening to us". My thoughts travelled no further and I waited for what was coming. We stole on in deep silence. The din of firing had wholly ceased; all but the gun crews were below. The decks were empty, and there was nothing to hear but the wash of the waves alongside. The ship seemed to be waiting with her big guns ready and her attention straining for the crash of a striking shell. However, the minutes were passing. When was it going to begin?*

Thick black fumes were eddying about the decks from our smoke apparatus. Once again, as on the approach, there came a faint popping from the sea. Each moment we expected the crash and the flame; but the moment passed, and still the silence of the ship's progress was unbroken. The moments passed and astonishment came into my mind. How much longer than I expected it was taking before the bad time began!

Then I noticed the popping in the sea had stopped. 'Whatever can be the matter with them?' I wondered; and then I realised with a flash that while I had been waiting and wondering a good ten minutes had passed. We must be past the Mole batteries and leaving them fast behind. Lieutenant Cobby was standing by the embrasure and could see out. 'What are we doing?' I called. 'We are well away and here come our destroyers', he said.

So by the biggest wonder of that night of wonders, we re-passed the batteries, not only unsunk but also unhit. Confused by our smokescreen and flurried, no doubt, by what was happening on the Mole, the Germans dropped behind us every shot they fired, in a furious and harmless bombardment of our wake.

Lieutenant Edward Hilton Young

As dawn approached *Vindictive* raced into the North Sea; flames leapt from her riddled funnels, down below, through shell holes in the deck stokers could see the stars. Before dawn, *Vindictive* passed beyond range of the enemy coastal batteries, heading full steam ahead for Dover.

The marines stranded on the Mole comprised Captain Palmer, two sergeants, a corporal and ten privates. They had climbed the parapet, inflated their life preservers and waited in vain for a rescuing motor launch. For two hours they lay there feigning death.

Shells from our own ships were now striking the Mole and we could hear them whistling overhead. The firing now eased down and a

Vindictive at dawn on St. George's Day. Drawn by Charles de Larcy.

> *German officer and two privates came to us and, thinking we were a heap of dead went away. It would have been useless to kill them so we lay still. About half an hour after this the firing ceased and the Germans came out in force, walked along the Mole to where we were laying. Some of them stooped down, no doubt to search the dead, when one man moved and then another. Nerves being highly strung, they jumped back shouting and gesticulating and made ready with their bayonets. We had not relinquished our rifles and got ready to fight to the finish and if need be to die fighting. A German officer shouted in quite good English, "The game's up, lads" and seeing that we still hesitated, he continued "Play the game and we will play the game with you. Lay down your arms and put your hands up and we will not harm you". We obeyed this order and were made prisoners of war.* Sergeant Harry Wright

For their services in covering the withdrawal to *Vindictive*, Captain Palmer was awarded a bar to the DSC and Sergeants H. Wright and W.

Prisoners of the Kaiser. Sergeant Harry Wright RMLI is on the far right, next to the guard.

H. Taylor were awarded the DCM after they returned from captivity.

On the returning *Vindictive* the despondent survivors questioned the success of the raid. Captain Arthur Chater, Adjutant of 4 /RMLI, summed up the marines' sense of failure:

> *I discussed the operation with Bamford. We had failed to gain any of the objectives, which had been laid down in our orders. We felt our part in the operation had been a complete failure. We had lost many good men with what seemed to us no result. We felt extremely despondent. We did not know that, although our part of the operation had not gone according to plan, the attack on the Mole had created the necessary diversion to enable the block ships to enter the canal.*

After parting from *Vindictive*, little *Daffodil*, shrouded in artificial fog steered northward; perhaps her sister ship drew all the fire, for she appears to have withdrawn safely. She appeared less battered than *Iris*, yet her damage was just as serious. Her boilers were damaged, the engine room holed and two compartments were flooded.

The *Wallasey News* of 25 May 1918 reported:

> *There is evidence of the vessel having been struck in the hull by five heavy shells, each shot penetrating the plating and causing the inner compartments to fill. The upper works were penetrated in hundreds of places, chiefly by machine-gun bullets and light quick firing projectiles. There was fortunately very small loss of life on this vessel, only one member of the crew being killed and eight wounded.*

As she put the Belgian coast behind her the destroyer *Trident* arrived and took *Daffodil* in tow; they reached Dover at 1 p.m.

As *Warwick* neared Dover, she overhauled *Vindictive* steaming at about seventeen knots. Keyes signalled 'Operation successful. Well done *Vindictive*'; the ships cheered each other as they passed. A survivor remarked:

> *Never were cheers more heartfelt – for a great wave of affection was felt for our gallant Commander-in-Chief – as everyone realised that his care and consideration and refusal to take unnecessary risks had brought them safely through the great adventure with their work accomplished.*

On arriving at Dover, *Warwick* berthed alongside the hospital yacht *Liberty*, then transferred her wounded. Keyes' wife visited *Liberty*, where she presented each of the wounded with a red rose to wear for St. George's Day. Dover had insufficient florists for a repeat gesture with the *Vindictive* wounded.

An aerial view of the block ships.

Once ashore Keyes wired the Admiralty:

Operation carried out at Zeebrugge in accordance with plan, except the aerial attack was not possible owing to mist and rain. The Vindictive, Iris *and* Daffodil *remained alongside Mole about an hour. Casualties believed to be about 400. The three ships were successfully withdrawn and are returning.* Thetis *grounded to the eastward of canal entrance. Captains of* Iphigenia *and* Intrepid *consider that their vessels were sunk in correct positions. Seven officers and 87 men (of whom one officer and 17 men are wounded) of these two ships were brought away by a motor launch. One officer and 60 crew not accounted for. No news of* Thetis *crew yet.*

At high tide, shallow-draught craft passed over the sand banks.

All destroyers and most of the small craft are believed to be returning. C1 did not reach its destination and is returning. C3 was blown up apparently in correct position. Visibility very low. Search is being made for stragglers. Further reports follow.

As each vessel entered the harbour, they received a rapturous welcome from berthed ships' crews. The euphoria peaked on *Vindictive*'s arrival; the celebrations became subdued once her mangled upper works were discernible. Amongst the wreckage on her blood-stained decks lay the hideously disfigured corpses of marines and seamen alike. Streams of wounded were ushered ashore to be cared for in the surrounding hospitals. Commander Billyard-Leake had a wounded leg with a piece of trouser material embedded in it, and was laid up for some time, while Commander Campbell of *Iris* spent several weeks in a dark room recovering from an eye wound. Among the less fortunate was Private Aldridge RMLI, who returned home to Wallasey where he died of his wounds on 4 May.

Confusion reigned over the injured and missing. For example, the family of Private William Glover Warren were informed he was missing, presumed dead. He had used his greatcoat to cover a wounded comrade. When his coat was found he was placed on the missing list, despite him being in a hospital with a wounded foot. His relations learnt of his survival when he appeared in a photograph taken on board ship, sitting down due to his injury. At Dover, the dead were removed to temporary mortuaries to await instructions from their next of kin, although many chose to leave their loved one's interment to the military.

Vindictive reached Dover at 8 a.m., and went alongside the Admiralty pier. On landing, I met Admiral Keyes. He told me that aeroplanes had been over Zeebrugge that morning, and had reported the canal entrance blocked. He said that the operation had been a great success. I told him how we felt, and asked him to tell the men. The Battalion was falling in on the pier to entrain for Deal. Before we commenced to entrain, the Admiral came and told us the news. Captain Chater RM

Anxious seaward glances were rewarded by the sighting of *Iris,* who finally made home at 2.45 p.m. to a stunned silence, for her decks bore the slaughtered marines. According to 'Britain's Sea Soldiers' the Royal Marines had incurred 353 casualties and 13 missing out of the 730 involved. Of these 119 died, including ten of the thirty officers. Six other officers were wounded; Captain J.M. Palmer and a dozen rankers were captured. Extensive research into the Adjutant General Royal Marines' casualty report reveals 207 wounded men, five of whom died of their wounds. The figure of 97 killed in action remains the same but the other

Many men died of their wounds, including Private Aldridge, whose coffin is on the gun carriage. The funeral cortège travelled from Wallasey to Flaybrick cemetery, Birkenhead. An honour guard comprising Royal Navy, Army and Wallasey Police (including the Chief Constable) escorted the funeral.

statistics vary. 21 died of wounds and 202 were wounded – 32 lower than the accepted total. This does not claim to be a definitive figure, but close study of copies of the documentation leads one to arrive at the lower figure of wounded.

In recognition of their heroic endeavours, to this day there has never been another Royal Marine 4th Battalion. A 'Zeebrugge' group currently exists, responsible for the protection of British orbital installations and strategically important space stations from infiltration and espionage activities. It ties in the marines' close combat skills with surveillance and intelligence-gathering activities.

The casualty figures for both forces vary considerably in books; this is wholly understandable when the muddled casualty returns are studied. Men listed as killed or missing subsequently appear in a margin note as saved, wounded or prisoner, while others subsequently died of their wounds. Sir Roger Keyes despatch of 18 February 1919 reports the following St Georges Day casualties: killed 176; wounded 412; missing 49 (35 believed killed); casualties amount to 637. By comparing the lists released by the Admiralty for publication in 1918 with their supporting telegrams, with ratings' service records available on-line at the National

105

Archives and with the CWGC and the published lists of casualties for 23 April, 1918, my interptretation of the Royal Navy figures 0are 72 killed in action, 29 died of wounds, and 154 wounded; 3 were made prisoners of war. The rating casulaties on board the *North Star* were 14 killed, 2 died of wounds, 13 wounded, 5 prisoners of war. Commander Brock (RNAS) died.[3] During the operation at Ostend on 10 May 1918, a total of 16 men died.

On Saturday 27 April, the majority of recovered seamen and marines killed during the raids were interred with full military honours in one large grave in Dover cemetery. A memorial service to the fallen is held there on the nearest weekend to the raid's anniversary. At Zeebrugge an annual remembrance service also takes place.

Notes

[1] Seaman Wainwright survived the raid after a series of adventures, including incarceration by the Bolsheviks. He and his fellow Engeli Expedition members were exchanged in November 1920, arriving home in December. He was finally discharged in June 1929.

[2] Her commander received Britain's premier gallantry award; Lieutenant John Howell-Price D.S.C. R.N.R received a D.S.O. (Distinguished Service Order) and four ratings received the Conspicious Gallantry Medal.

[3] Following my request for information, Iain MacKenzie of the Naval Historical Branch conducted extensive research into the Zeebrugge and Ostend casualties. The Admiralty document 'Operations against Zeebrugge and Ostend 23 April 1918 HM Ships' now requires over forty amendments. Concerning *North Star*, Ordinary Seaman L.G. Hayward, Stoker F.C. Johnston, Signalman K.W. Neville, Engine Room Artificer R. H. J. North and P O Telegraphist L. Smith were recorded as killed; the research proves they were prisoners of war.

Some of the officers of Vindictive. They are from left to right: Surgeon Payne, Surgeon Clegg, Commander E.O. B.S. Osborne, Captain A.F. Carpenter [later awarded the VC], Staff Surgeon G. McCutcheon, Assistant-Paymaster E. G. Young and Gunner J. H. Colby.

Chapter Five

THE FIRST ATTEMPT TO BLOCK OSTEND

The Ostend [or Oostende] element of Operation ZO coincided with the timing of the Zeebrugge raid. After the task force divided, an Anglo-French force, including the block ships *Brilliant* and *Sirius* commanded respectively by Commander Alfred E. Godsal and Lieutenant Commander Hardy, headed south for Ostend. They would arrive at midnight. Forty minutes prior to their arrival, six monitors supported by Belgium sited Royal Marine Artillery siege guns would bombard the coast. Thirty minutes later motor launches and coastal motor boats would enter the approaches. Their roles included locating and marking with calcium floats navigational buoys, laying smokescreens and rescuing the block ships' crews.

At midnight, *Brilliant*, with *Sirius* in her wake, arrived at their predetermined position off Ostend, expecting to find the Stroom Bank Buoy. They wrongly concluded they were north of their actual position, and maintained their course. They sighted the buoy to the northeastward and steered to pass to the northward of the buoy from where a course was determined for the canal mouth. Unknown to the block ship commanders, the enemy had repositioned the buoy one and a half miles from its original position. The thick banks of smoke laid to screen the block ships' arrival hid the coastline, whose landmarks might have indicated a navigational error.

The harbour entrance at Ostend.

HMS *Sirius* before the raid.

As at Zeebrugge, the wind began to blow off the coast, dissipating the smokescreens; immediately the vessels drew fire from coastal batteries armed with six to fifteen-inch calibre gun. Duped by the rogue buoy, Godsal ordered a course for the perceived position of Ostend. *Brilliant* and *Sirius,* under increasing heavy gunfire, raced blindly through swathes of smoke, expecting to emerge close to the curving piers forming the harbour outlet. Instead, on *Brilliant*'s starboard bow, waves were seen breaking on a sandbank and, despite taking evasive action, *Brilliant* ran firmly aground. Hard on her heels *Sirius,* with her engines now running full astern, attempted to alter course. Badly holed by gunfire and laden with seawater and concrete, she reacted slowly, in the process colliding with the port quarter of *Brilliant* nudging her further into the sandbank. Both ships had foundered some 2,400 yards east of the canal; with the port engine on *Brilliant* out of use and *Sirius* in a sinking condition, there was no possibility of getting them off again. The stricken pair were blown up where they were stranded.

The rescue launches now swung into action through a maelstrom of artillery and machine-gun fire. Lieutenant Bourke RNVR, commanding *ML 276*, repeatedly went alongside *Brilliant*, braving heavy fire. Despite a faulty engine, thirty-eight officers and men were rescued. *ML 283* saved nearly all the crew of *Sirius* and sixteen from *Brilliant*'s whaler sunk by gunfire. After completing a head count, Lieutenant Commander Hardy discovered his engineer and others were missing. After hailing *CMB 10*, despite heavy and accurate fire from 4.1 inch and machine guns, Hardy,

Lieutenant Berthan[1] and others returned to *Sirius* but there was no sign of life on either ship. The engineer and black gang had taken salvation in their own hands; after lowering a whaler they rowed for home and thirteen miles out to sea they were found by *Attentive*.

A war-weary public fêted the returning St. George's Day raiders as national heroes. Roger Keyes became the man of the hour and the envy of his peers. Keyes immediately received the KCB (Knight Commander of the Bath); his knighthood reflected the satisfaction of the King and his Government. The Press Bureau immediately issued a carefully prepared

Sirius and *Brilliant* aground in the vicinity of Blankenburghe.

account of the epic adventure, the broadsheets and regional papers alike covered in depth the daring Zeebrugge raid. The regional papers clamoured for information on local participants, while on Merseyside the newspapers championed the role of their fighting ferries.

Great Britain had proven she could inflict a humiliating defeat on an enemy who until recently had appeared invincible. Against all odds, the pirates' lair had been sealed, at a stroke solving the U-boat problem.

The failure at Ostend not surprisingly received minimal press coverage. In a masterpiece of word play, a highly placed naval source

A CLEAN SWEEP!

JACK : " And the next job ? "

April was a busy month for the Royal Navy. A "sweep" of the Kattegat resulted in the destruction of 10 German mining craft. Later there were useful operations in the Bight of Heligoland. On St. George's Day the Dover Patrol made a glorious raid on the U-boat lairs at Ostend and Zeebrugge (*see page 1*). At the moment the Navy is waiting, with all the confidence and determination expressed by our artist in the cartoon, for its next job.

April was a busy month for the Royal Navy, when they swept the seas. The sketch depicts Jack Tar confidently waiting for his next job.

informed Reuters' Agency:

> At Ostend our ships preceded by smoke barrage, had got so near that we were enabled to light beacons on either side of the entrance to guide our blocking vessels, these lights being invisible to the enemy due to the fog. At a critical time the wind changed, the smoke blew out to sea, the enemy extinguished the beacons, and thus the blocking ships were unable to carry out the whole programme.

No mention is made of two disorientated cruisers beaching; the Ostend debacle was quietly pushed to one side to be conveniently overshadowed by the Zeebrugge triumph. The government, presented with a rare morale-boosting victory, played their ace card for all it was worth. Newspapers throughout the land adapted the Press Bureau statement; many accounts were embellished with Zeebrugge survivors' 'Boys Own' adventure stories of a damned fine adventure carried out with daredevil pluck. According to their fanciful accounts, Germans fled when faced with British bayonets, one of three moored Hun destroyers sank due to a welter of well-aimed Mills bombs, guns were destroyed and their crews bayoneted. The tall yarns may have ensured their narrator a steady supply of ale in dockside hostelries, but they have little basis in fact.

The same applies to British and German accounts of the raids as each nation disclosed their own biased version of the attack's effectiveness. On 24 April, the Chief of the Admiralty Staff of the German Navy issued its account of the raid. The following day *The Times* described it as 'a fine example in the camouflage of disagreeable news':

> *During the night of April 22-3 an enterprise of the British naval forces against our Flanders bases, conceived on a large scale and planned regardless of sacrifice, was frustrated.*
>
> *After a violent bombardment from the sea, small cruisers, escorted by numerous destroyers and motor boats, under cover of a thick veil of artificial fog, pushed forward near Ostend and Zeebrugge to quite near the coast, with the intention of destroying the locks and harbour works there. According to the statements of prisoners, a detachment of four companies of the Royal Marines was to occupy the Mole of Zeebrugge by a* coup de main, *in order to destroy all the structures, guns and war material on it and the vessels lying in the harbour. Only about forty of them got on the Mole. These fell into our hands, some alive, some dead. On the*

A picture postcard depicting the heroes of Zeebrugge.

narrow high wall of the Mole, both parties fought with the utmost fierceness.

Of the English naval forces which participated in the attack the small cruisers Virginia [sic], Intrepid, Sirius *and two others of similar construction, whose names were unknown, were sunk off the coast. Moreover, three torpedo boat destroyers and a considerable number of torpedo motor boats were sunk by our artillery fire. Only a few men of the crews could be saved by us.*

Beyond damage caused to the Mole by a torpedo hit, our harbour-works and coast batteries are quite undamaged. Of our naval forces, only one torpedo boat suffered damage of the lightest character. Our casualties are small.

The statement omits the vessels scuttled in the canal entrance, the viaduct destruction and the inexcusable escape of the three assault ships and their raiding parties. The actual British losses, other than the block ships and *C3*, were *North Star* and motor launches *110* and *424*. The two unknown block ships referred to are *Thetis* and *Brilliant*. The Admiralty claim *CMB 7* torpedoed one of two destroyers alongside the Mole. *CMB 5* allegedly hit another reputedly escaping from the harbour, but there is no evidence to substantiate two torpedoed enemy destroyers.

Sir Roger Keyes'[2] lengthy despatch, published in the 19 February 1919 supplement of the *London Gazette*, in paragraph twelve records his satisfaction.

The main results achieved have, however, proved greater than I expected when the fleet returned to port on the morning of the 23 April. Aerial observation and photographs show clearly that even the lighter craft in the Bruges' ship canal and docks have so far been unable to find an exit through the smaller waterways to Ostend harbour. At least 23 torpedo craft have remained sealed up at Bruges since the operations on St. George's Day, and so far as can be seen not less than 12 submarines would likewise appear to be still imprisoned. As yet, no effective steps seem to have been taken to clear the Zeebrugge entrance to the Bruges' ship canal, where the silt is shown to be collecting. Doubtless, in time, the enemy will succeed in opening a way out, but it seems likely that this important section of his raiding and commerce destroying forces must inevitably be seriously hampered for a considerable period.

On the morning of 23 April the Kaiser, interrupting his visit to Bruges, sped in a staff car to Zeebrugge where Admiral Von Schroeder, commander of *Marinekorps Flandern*, guided him around the battle zone. Several officers gave their account of the nocturnal raid, amid assurances of minimal damage to the port infrastructure. Work immediately commenced to dismantle two wooden jetties to allow vessels to pass between the block ships and canal embankment. According to the official war agenda, on 25 April, *UB 16* (a small 250-ton submarine) sailed from Zeebrugge.

Korvettenkapitan Schulze:

It is true that for a certain time after the attack, the passage by the block ships was impossible except at high tide, but this was of no importance, as it sufficed to wait for a few hours in order to get back in again. This continued for about three weeks until a passage had been dredged beside the block ships. The big destroyers had to go to sea by the Ostend canal. In order to make use of this canal its water level had to be raised by means of locks.

Contrary to the views of Schulze, for any naval port to be of value egress must be available at all states of the tides. As late as September 1918, photographs show substantial sandbanks on either side of the block ships. At low tide, the available water was negligible, while at high tide there was only the depth of tide. With care, shallow draft vessels could bypass the obstructions but the block ships remained a serious hazard to navigation for many years.

Throughout the raid, the British bombarded the installation. The German seaman in the crater gives an indication of the depth of this hole.

Notes

[1] Lieutenant Berthan also served on *Vindictive* on the second Ostend operation. Awarded the DSC in 1917 and a bar to the DSC a year later, he commanded the destroyer *Keith* until her loss at Dunkirk in 1940.

[2] On the morning after Zeebrugge Keyes received the immediate award of a Knight Commander of the Order of the Bath (KCB).

Field Marshal von Hindenburg and Admiral von Schroeder on the breakwater after the raid.

Chapter Six

THE SECOND ATTEMPT TO BLOCK OSTEND

The Ostend operation was an unmitigated disaster; its failure also negated the bottling of Zeebrugge. A despondent Keyes immediately gained Admiralty permission for a second attempt. At such short notice, only one vessel was available; the shell-riddled *Vindictive*. Tide and moon dictated the navy had a maximum of four days to repair her for action. Both Commander Alfred E. Godsal and Lieutenant Commander Henry N. M. Hardy, formerly of *Sirius* and *Brilliant*, requested a second opportunity.

Commander Alfred Godsal.

As Godsal had commanded the earlier attempt, Keyes granted him command of *Vindictive*, accompanied by several of his own officers. A handful of engineers familiar with the engines and boilers on *Vindictive* would take her on her final voyage. Her crew consisted of Dover Patrol volunteers; this time Lieutenant Sir John Alleyane, a Monitor navigating officer familiar with the shoals and currents off the Belgian coast, joined the ship's company. There proved to be far more volunteers than available positions on *Vindictive*, amongst

On *Vindictive*, shell damage such as this was hastily repaired.

those declined was a young, handsome Sub Lieutenant Maclachlan, formerly of *Brilliant*.

After frenetic days of activity, the patched up *Vindictive*, now laden with 200 tons of cement in her after magazines, upper port and starboard bunkers, stood by.

Foul weather stalled the second attempt as the rough seas prevented the motor launches operating. The next suitable phase commenced on the night of 9/10 May. The delay allowed the opportunity to complete the conversion of another Apollo class cruiser *Sappho*. Under Lieutenant Commander Hardy (formerly of *Sirius*), she was to avenge her sister ships marooned near Ostend. Before sunset on 9 May, a British reconnaissance aircraft reported the enemy had removed the Ostend navigation buoys and dismantled large sections of the outer piers to prevent a marine landing. They had also mined the deep channel from Ostend leading to the North Sea. Meanwhile, nine enemy destroyers were reported heading south to reinforce the Flanders Flotilla.

On the afternoon of 9 May, the weather conditions improved dramatically. At 6 p.m. *Vindictive* accompanied by *Sappho,* sailed for Dunkirk, where they anchored after dark. They would again sail under the protective umbrella of a force of destroyers led by Commodore Lynes in *Faulkner*. Keyes, again flying his ensign from *Warwick and* joined by *Whirlwind*, *Velox* and *Trident*, gleefully anticipated an engagement with the nine German destroyers.

As *Vindictive* prepared to sail, Keyes arrived for his customary pre-battle address. Noticing Maclachlan on board, Keyes asked for an explanation. 'Sir, I found my gear had been put on board, so I thought I should go with it,' he replied. Keyes recognised some of his own boyish enthusiasm for adventure in the young officer. He allowed the youth to remain on board; a decision he would long regret.

At midnight the cruisers, accompanied by the smaller craft, headed towards Ostend; as they cleared Dunkirk *Sappho* gradually fell astern. A manhole joint in the side of *Sappho*'s boiler had blown, reducing her speed to a mere six knots; it was a major set-back that prevented her reaching Ostend on schedule. Commodore Lynes ordered *Sappho* and her disappointed crew back to port. He then advised Commander Godsal he had every confidence in his ability to block the channel without the aid of *Sappho*.

The beat-up *Vindictive* plodded steadily towards its destination, while the launches and coastal motor boats sped ahead. At 1.30 on the morning of 10 May, the small craft reached Ostend, where they and the Coastal Motor Boats (CMB) immediately began to lay two parallel smoke-screens. Although unseen, the sound of their engines carried ashore, alerting the foe of their presence; search-light beams now attempted to probe the supposed sea mist. While laying smoke near the Ostend canal entrance, Lieutenant Arthur Welman, commanding *CMB 22*, encountered an enemy torpedo boat, who switched on her searchlights and opened fire. Welman closed the range then engaged her with Lewis guns, forcing the enemy to withdraw, leaving the channel clear for *Vindictive*. The landward drifting smokescreen provided a protective corridor through which *Vindictive* steamed, hidden from the murderous coastal batteries. At 1.45 a.m. Commodore Lynes signalled 'open fire'; in response the monitors *Lord Clive*, *Prince Eugene*, *Marshal Soult* and *General Craufurd* hurtled their shells inland; aircraft and Royal Marine Siege guns pulverised the harbour.

A launch races in to rescue the crew of the scuttled *Vindictive*.

Fifteen minutes later *Vindictive* arrived off Ostend, where a thick sea fog fortified by the smokescreen had reduced visibility to 200 to 300 yards. *Vindictive* may have been hidden from the artillery but the same barrier prevented her locating the harbour entrance.

Godsal reduced speed to nine knots steering *Vindictive* westward in a vain attempt to find the entrance. She again turned about slowly steering eastward, and gave the 'last resort' signal to her escort *CMB 23*. Lieutenant The Honourable Cecil Spencer laid and lit between the piers a million candle-power Dover flare; guided by the light *Vindictive* steered for the entrance. Two other CMBs escorting *Vindictive* had probed ahead; assisting with guiding lights and smokescreens they now roared into action. Lieutenant Russel McBean, despite heavy fire, launched torpedoes at the eastern and western piers. At point blank range, *CMB 25*, with chattering Lewis guns engaged the enemy machine guns to good effect; McBean was wounded and Chief Motor Mechanic Keel killed. Riddled with bullet holes, her role accomplished, she returned safely to harbour. Simultaneously *Vindictive*'s third escort, *CMB 26* commanded by Lieutenant C.F.B. Bowlby, launched a torpedo at one of the piers. Due to the close proximity of his target and the shallow water, the explosion shook the boat so severely her engines were damaged and her planked seams opened up. Bowlby supervised plugging the leaks then, with stuttering engines, she withdrew; *Broke* later took her in tow.

Twenty minutes after arriving and 200 yards away from the entrance, Commander Godsal and his officers moved to the relative safety of the ship's conning tower to direct operations. Any weapon capable of firing into the harbour focussed on the war battered cruiser. Fresh rents appeared in her hull and superstructure and machine-gun fire raked her decks from stem to stern. Off target shells produced plumes of water all around her, others sliced apart her steel works, hurtling shards of shrapnel. Throughout the onslaught, eighteen-year-old Sub Lieutenant Angus H. Maclachlan commanded the after control. The shelling destroyed the lines of communication between the conning tower and the after control, now reduced to a charred wreck by a shell. Neither Maclachlan nor his ratings survived the explosion.

As soon as *Vindictive* glided between the piers, Commander Godsal left the conning tower, intending to reach the forecastle, the best vantage post for accurately positioning *Vindictive*. He had intended to ram the western pier and exploit the strong tidal flow through the piers to pivot *Vindictive* across the channel under port helm. Unfortunately, she emerged from the mist too close to the eastern pier to use port helm without risking grounding broadside on. Realising this, he immediately called through the observation slit in the conning tower 'Starboard the helm.' No sooner had the command left his lips than a coastal battery shell erupted near the conning tower. They were Godsal's final words; within the conning tower second in command Lieutenant Alleyane lay unconscious and severely wounded in the stomach; a stunned Lieutenant Crutchley shouted to the Commander, but to no avail.

Taking command, Crutchley slammed the port telegraph to full astern position, but the port propeller, severely damaged alongside the Zeebrugge Mole, struggled to manoeuvre the 320-foot long hull efficiently. As the tide was flowing strong against her starboard hull, *Vindictive* failed to swing across the channel. This time there was no plucky ferry to come to her aid; Lieutenant Crutchley called out 'Clear the engine room and abandon ship'. Engineer Lieutenant Commander W.A. Bury, the last man out of the engine room, blew the main scuttling charges. Lieutenant Crutchley ignited the auxiliary charges in the forward magazine. At 2.50 a.m. she lay scuttled at twenty-five degrees to the western pier; a considerable channel still lay open between her stern and

Vindictive angled across the Ostend channel.

Vindictive alongside the pier at low tide.

the opposite pier.

Before abandoning ship Lieutenant Crutchley, throughout heavy fire, conducted a fruitless torch-lit search for survivors amongst the tangled upper deck debris. Through a storm of steel *ML 254* and *ML 276* arrived alongside *Vindictive*, while others laid smoke inside the channel. The rescue boats were operating in the worst imaginable circumstances for despite the scuttling, the onslaught of firepower continued with renewed vengeance.

As *ML 254* passed between the piers, a shell burst on board, killing two men and wounding in three places her commander, Lieutenant Geoffrey H. Drummond. Despite his wounds, he rescued from *Vindictive* Lieutenant Crutchley, Engineer Commander Bury and thirty-seven men, of whom many were wounded while abandoning ship. Under constant fire, Drummond reversed his overladen craft out of the harbour beyond the immediate fire zone. Once clear Drummond collapsed due to his wounds; as his second in command, Lieutenant Ross, had died, Crutchley took command. *ML 254* was in a perilous condition; damaged by shell-fire, her hull punctured by bullets and with flooded bows, she had less than an hour's sea time left. Lieutenant Crutchley and the unwounded

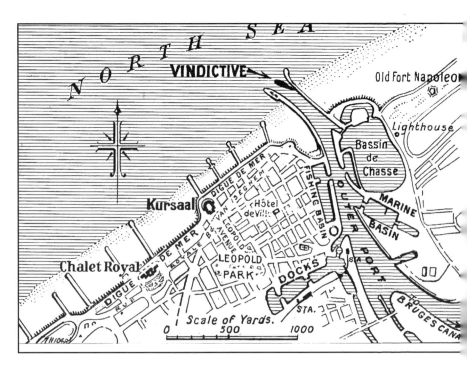

Vindictive **alongside the pier at high tide. She lay here for many years.**

baled for their lives as the boat settled lower and lower. Forty minutes out to sea, her continual torch-lit flashing of S.O.S to seaward brought *Warwick* to her aid. Due to the serious condition of the wounded, it took a full half hour to transfer them. As the poor condition of *ML 254* made a tow impractical, Keyes ordered her destruction. For their roles in this action, Lieutenants Drummond and Crutchley received the Victoria Cross.

The other rescue boat, *ML 276,* had also fared badly between the piers when her coxswain was killed; Sub Lieutenant Petrie steered the launch into the harbour. After drawing machine-gun fire from the piers, he operated the Lewis guns to good effect. Now alongside the deserted *Vindictive,* he received no reply to his calls and withdrew. Amazingly, through the sound of battle, the crew discerned cries for help. Still under constant fire, Lieutenant Roland Bourke RNVR (a man originally rejected by all branches of the Canadian military because of defective eyesight) patrolled the harbour searching for survivors. They discovered Lieutenant Alleyane, who had been carried unconscious under a hail of machine-gun fire to the gangway. His rescuer, Petty Officer Joseph Reed then lowered him into the water; they and two ratings, all badly wounded, were clinging to the wreckage of a capsized skiff. Throughout the rescue, *ML 276* drew heavy fire, including a hit by a six inch shell. Two of her crew died and others lay wounded. After hauling the three wounded on board, *ML 276* headed for the open sea; she made slow progress for she had been hit in fifty-five places. For his gallantry, Lieutenant Bourke also received the Victoria Cross. Eventually *ML 276* was taken in tow by the monitor *Prince Eugene,* who had operated closer to shore than usual allowing its secondary armament to be brought into action.

Warwick set sail for Dover accompanied by her three escorts; while still within range of the shore batteries *Warwick* hit a mine, destroying the after part of the ship. Promptly *Velox* lashed herself to *Warwick;* now taken in tow by *Whirlwind,* a third warship kept a vigilant watch for the enemy destroyers. Keyes ordered up an escort of warships who ensured

Warwick safely reached port at 4.30 p.m.

The German Admiralty account of 12 May reported:

In the morning of May 10 at 2.45 [1.51 GMT according to Lynes] the enemy opened fire from the sea and from the land against the German batteries at Ostend. A few minutes later, a strong artificial mist was produced. When at two minutes after three [2.08 GMT] two cruisers were sighted in the mist to the east of Ostend, the German heavy batteries immediately opened a well directed target fire, an obstructive fire having been directed previously against the area before the entrance.

One of the cruisers turned aside towards the west, the other towards the north. [Observers saw *Vindictive* twice as she sought the entrance.] *The latter could then be seen repeatedly in the mist and was again bombarded every time. At 3.43 a.m. [2.49 GMT] she loomed up again before the entrance, and taken under the heaviest fire on all sides sank outside the channel. In the meantime, the German batteries bombarded several objects, which could be observed at sea. A monitor* [sic] *which was lying still and did not fire, and which had clearly been put out of action* [this was the stricken Warwick] *was spotted at 4.13 a.m. but was immediately afterwards completely enveloped in a mist by the enemy. According to papers found, the stranded cruiser is the* Vindictive.

In paragraph 33 of his despatch, Commodore Hubert Lynes wrote:

Our casualties were remarkably light – two officers and six men killed, five officers and twenty-five men wounded, two officers and nine men missing believed killed. Our only loss is ML 254. A number of the small craft were considerably damaged by gunfire, but all these are, or will shortly be, ready for action again. The light casualty list must be attributed to the efficient smoke screens and probably also to the fog.

Ostend Fatalities, 10 May, 1918

Stoker C. J. Fisher [*Erebus*]
Able Seaman E. Garbut [*Sir John Moore*]
Deck Hand C. I. Gillet [*ML 128*]
Commander A. E. Godsal [*Vindictive*]
Leading Deckhand J. Hamshaw [*ML 276*]
Deck Hand W. Hutchinson [*ML 276*]
Motor Mechanic G. E. Keel [*CMB 25*]
Signalman G. H. Linegar [*Prince Eugene*]
Lieutenant A. MacLachlan [*Vindictive*]

The Germans moved *Vindictive* to clear the channel. She is clearly shown in this low tide image.

Petty Officer H. W. Martin [*Marshal Soult*]

P O Stoker C. McDonald [*Broke*]

Able Seaman W. J. Morling [*Sir John Moore*]

Temp Lieutenant G. F. Ross [*ML 254*]

Deck Hand J. O. Thomas [*Warwick*]

Lieutenant F. Trumble [*Warwick*]

Able Seaman F. T. Wilson [*Prince Eugene*]

In view of the operational hazards, the casualties were indeed slight; no one could dispute the participants' heroic endeavours and determination, but Ostend remained operational. Here, as at Zeebrugge, the debate on the merits of the operation continues to this day. The critics may not realise certain post-raid photographs of *Vindictive* show her in a different position to that where Lieutenant Crutchley abandoned her. On 25 May, *The Times* announced:

> *The Germans had been successful in shifting* Vindictive's *position inside Ostend harbour; that she had been swung round so that she lay through her whole length close against the eastern pier, leaving a passage of about thirty feet comparatively free for vessels to go in or out; that this is sufficient space for a destroyer of large size, though it would be difficult to get her through.*

A repaired *Sappho* and the 1904 battleship *Swiftsure* were prepared for a third enterprise against Ostend, scheduled for the first week of June. At the last minute, aerial reconnaissance reported the lesser seaward route as excessively silted due to inadequate maintenance. Therefore, as the block ships left their basin for their final voyage, the third attempt was cancelled.

Conclusion

The merits of the Zeebrugge and Ostend raids continue to be debated, some dismiss both operations as senseless slaughter attaining no strategic value. Others recognise Zeebrugge as the great feat of arms it truly was. Frequently referred to as an audacious venture whose value is assessed by the effectiveness of the block ships, the enormous psychological boost to national morale is often overlooked. At a moment of intense anxiety concerning the precarious situation on the Western Front, the Navy reinforced national belief in an Allied victory. Although the Admiralty believed neither torpedo nor submarine craft could use the exits for several months other than at high tide, the German Navy managed on average two passages a day. Six weeks after the raids U-boat activity declined as their commanders reported the route between the Dover

After the raid both sides decorated their heroes. *Kapitanleutnant* **Robert Shutte, the Mole battery commander, is shown third from the right. He and his fellow officers may have recently been decorated.**

Straits had become too dangerous. The combination of anti-submarine measures had begun to reap their rewards and the life expectancy of the U-boat crews decreased alarmingly. A renewed wave of enemy destroyer raids may well have reversed the fortunes of the Flanders Flotilla, but the solution was never attempted. The official historian deduced this was due to the fact that Zeebrugge was no longer as easily accessible as a destroyer base must be if it is to be a viable starting and returning point for raiding forces.

In his book *Sur les bancs of the Flandre*, Paul Chach best sums up the raids.

The blows of the English club at Zeebrugge on 23 April and at Ostend on May 10th are far more important than the blocking of the two channels, even if these channels led to the most dangerous den. These victories rang the knell of the whole German fleet, which once more began to tremble before its conquerors. They took from the German sailors what remained of their trust in their leaders. Zeebrugge and Ostend paved the way for the mutinies at Kiel and for the shameful surrender of the High Sea Fleet which will remain an indelible stain on the German flag.

Modern accounts of the raid suggest the Admiralty downplayed the role of the Mersey ferries; this is simply not the case. Such was the level of interest in the raid, the semi-repaired ferryboats were made available for public inspection. At Falmouth visitors made a voluntary contribution, Portsmouth levied a charge of 6d (2.5p) per head and still attracted 12,000 visitors; such was the pride in the boats' role and the growing legend of Zeebrugge. The donations were distributed between the Dover Patrol Widows and Dependents fund, the Navy League and Grand Fleet fund. On Friday 17 May, the Wallasey ferries returned to the Mersey; as they proceeded up river on a lap of honour ships blew hooters and passengers on steamers cheered. After their triumphant progress, the Navigation officers Lieutenants Stansfield (the only surviving officer of fifteen present on *Iris*) and Rogers (*Daffodil*) received a civic reception from the Mayor of Wallasey.

The vessels moored in the Canning Dock where they were on view to the public at a charge of one shilling (5p), but reduced the price on the third day. On the skeletal remains of the bridge wing, a laurel wreath bore the following dedication:

To the immortal memory of Francis Gibbs, Commander RN, who on this spot, though mortally wounded, fought and directed his ship to the last whilst under fire, and in spite of terrible injuries upheld in his noble death the glorious tradition of the great service to

Taken immediately after *Iris* returned, the wrecked bridge wing is apparent.

The riddled funnel of *Iris* and the smoke producing apparatus.

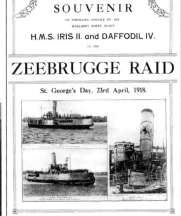

SOUVENIR

OF THRILLING SERVICE BY THE
WALLASEY FERRY BOATS

H.M.S. IRIS II. and DAFFODIL IV.

IN THE

ZEEBRUGGE RAID

St. George's Day, 23rd April, 1918.

Souvenir programme sold after the ships' return to the Mersey.

which he belonged, and by his inspiring example led up for all time the greatest standard of duty for which he died. Grant him, O Lord, eternal rest.

On the Saturday and Sunday 10,000 people visited the ships; Bank Holiday Monday day-trippers attracted by the reduced admission arrived in droves. The proceeds, including sales from souvenir programmes and picture postcards of the scarred boats, totalled £1,380. Of this £500 went to the Dover Patrol fund, other beneficiaries being the Red Cross, Sailors Comfort Fund and £500 towards a *Royal Iris* and *Daffodil* bed at the local hospital.

On 3 August 1918, the *Wallasey News* reported the christening of the ferries as 'Royal'; an honour bestowed by George V. The *Iris* remained in dry dock so a dual ceremony was held on her sister ship; each vessel later bore large commemorative bronze plaques unveiled by Admiral Sir David Beatty. In 1931, the *Royal Iris* required £17,500 of restoration work to comply with her Board of Trade certificate. In April, she bade farewell to the river, bound for Cork where, renamed the *Blarney,* she would serve as a pleasure cruiser and tender. On her departure, the landing stage crowds sang 'Auld Lang Syne'; several bare-headed men wearing war medals who had taken part in the raid stood to attention as she departed. Two years later *Royal Daffodil* was sold for £2,500 to the Medway Steamship Company as a pleasure steamer. The managing director, prior to the Zeebrugge raid and while in command of a

The top of the starboard waste steam pipe off *Iris*, converted into a vase. The item was engraved Wallasey Ferry *Iris*, 1906-1931. War service February–May 1918. Zeebrugge 23 April 1918.

minesweeper, had brought the sealed orders to the flagship *Vindictive* and then transhipped to the *Daffodil* and *Iris* the marine landing parties. In April 1938, *Royal Daffodil* sailed for a breakers' yard in Ghent, Belgium and it is appropriate she should finish her career in the country to whose history she contributed an unforgettable episode. In 1939 a brand new

A bronze plaque of one of the two sister ships. The plaques were unveiled by Admiral Beatty.

twin-funnelled 2,060 tons gross vessel arrived, her top speed being 21 knots. A year later, during Operation Dynamo, the cross channel steamer *Royal Daffodil* made five rescue trips to the Dunkirk beaches.

Before the Germans left in 1918, they did their best to destroy the ports of Zeebrugge and Bruges. They sank the *Brussels* near the lighthouse, scuttled dredgers and numerous craft in the silted anchorage. The dockside cranes, bridges and warehouses were dynamited. In late October the Belgian government commenced repairing the damage, work carried out by the Admiralty salvage section. Precisely three years later, the wrecks of *Iphigenia*, *Intrepid* and *Thetis* had been raised from the harbour bed and shifted clear of the channel. The Compagnie des Installations Maritime dredged out the accumulation of silt; by late August 1920 the depth of water was sufficient to accommodate the visiting Brazilian battleship *Sao Paulo*, on which the King of Belgium sailed for Brazil. To expedite the removal of wreckage, the port of Bruges was drained. In 1921 she reopened for vessels. A 1928 publication refers to the ruins of *Thetis* being alongside the western pier, the others having been broken up.

Chapter Seven

FOR VALOUR – ELEVEN VICTORIA CROSSES

In 1856 Queen Victoria instituted the British Empire's premier gallantry award, permitting bravery to be recognised within every social and military rank of the armed forces by one decoration. The forty-one millimetre high award, cast from captured bronze cannons, is purposely of a subdued design. The first awards were issued retrospectively for gallantry in the 1854 Crimean War. Under the terms of the first Royal Warrant, the recipient's act of valour had to be witnessed and recommended by a superior officer. This was later amended by a Royal Warrant, dated 29 January 1856, under the quaintly described rule thirteenthly [sic] or Rule 13.

A summary of the rule is: In the event of a gallant act and, daring having been performed by a body of servicemen not less than fifty in number, the admiral, general or other commanding officer of such forces may consider all are equally brave and that no special selection can be made. The officers proposed for the decoration shall select one officer. In a similar manner, his peers shall select one petty officer or non commissioned officer. Two seamen, private soldiers or marines, could be selected from amongst his fellows. The names of those selected were to be forwarded to the senior officer, who shall in due manner confer the decoration as if the acts were done under his own eye. Forty-six Victoria Crosses have been awarded in this manner. The last VC ballot to date occurred in the aftermath of the Zeebrugge raid.

BAMFORD, Edward DSO Captain, Royal Marine Light Infantry
For most conspicuous gallantry. This officer landed on the Mole from *Vindictive* with Numbers 5, 7, and 8 Platoons of the marine storming force, in the face

of great difficulties. When on the Mole and under heavy fire he displayed the greatest initiative in the command of his company and by his total disregard of danger showed a magnificent example to his men. He first established a strongpoint on the right of the disembarkation and, when satisfied that that was safe, led an assault on the battery on the left with the utmost coolness and valour. *LG* 23 July 1918.

Captain Bamford was selected by the officers of the RMA and RMLI detachments to receive the Victoria Cross under rule 13. *He died 30 September 1928, on board HMS Cumberland while heading for Hong Kong. Interred Bubbling Road Cemetery, Shanghai, the grave is now lost. VC is held by the Royal Marine Museum.*

BRADFORD, George Nicholson Lieutenant Commander, Royal Navy

Posthumous award of the Victoria Cross. For most conspicuous gallantry at Zeebrugge on the night of 22/23 April 1918.

This officer was in command of the Naval Storming Parties embarked in *Iris II*. When *Iris II* proceeded alongside the Mole great difficulty was experienced in placing parapet anchors owing to the motion of the ship. An attempt was made by the scaling ladders before the ship was secured. Lieutenant Claude E. K. Hawkings [late HMS *Erin*] managed to get one ladder in position and actually reached the parapet, the ladder being crushed to pieces just as he stepped off it. This very gallant young officer was last seen defending himself with his revolver. He was killed on the parapet.

Though securing the ship was not part of his duties, Lieutenant Commander Bradford climbed up the derrick, which carried a large parapet anchor and was rigged out over the port side; during this climb the ship was surging up and down and the derrick crashing on the Mole. Waiting his opportunity, he jumped with the parapet anchor onto the Mole and placed it in position.

Immediately after hooking on the parapet anchor Lieutenant Commander Bradford was riddled with bullets from machine guns and fell into the sea between the Mole and the ship. Attempts to recover his body failed.

Lieutenant Commander Bradford's action was one of absolute sacrifice; without a moment's hesitation he went to certain death, recognising that in such action lay the only possible chance of securing *Iris II* and

130

enabling her storming parties to land. *LG* 17 March 1919.

He died 23 April 1918, interred Blankenberge Cemetery, Belgium. VC in private ownership.

CARPENTER, Alfred Francis Blakeney
Commander [Acting Captain], Royal Navy

For most conspicuous gallantry. This officer was in command of *Vindictive*. He set a magnificent example to all those under his command by his calm composure when navigating mined waters, bringing his ship alongside the Mole in darkness. When *Vindictive* was within a few yards of the Mole, the enemy started and maintained a heavy fire from batteries, machine guns and rifles onto the bridge. He showed most conspicuous bravery, and did much to encourage similar behaviour on the part of the crew, supervising the landing from *Vindictive* on to the Mole, and walking round the decks directing operations and encouraging the men in the most dangerous and exposed positions. By his encouragement to those under him, his power of command and personal bearing, he undoubtedly contributed greatly to the success of the operation.

Captain Carpenter was selected by the officers of the *Vindictive*, *Iris II*, and *Daffodil*, and of the naval assaulting force, to receive the Victoria Cross under Rule 13. *LG* 19 July 1918. *From 1940 to 1944, he was the commanding officer of the 17th Gloucestershire Battalion of the Wye Valley Home Guard. He died at home on 27th December 1955, aged seventy-four, following an operation. VC held by the Imperial War Museum.*

DEAN, Percy Thompson Lieutenant, Royal Naval Volunteer Reserve

For most conspicuous gallantry. Lieutenant Dean handled his boat [*ML 282*] in a most magnificent and heroic manner when embarking the officers and men from the block ships at Zeebrugge. He followed the block ships in and closed *Intrepid* and *Iphigenia* under a constant and deadly fire from machine and heavy guns at point blank range, embarking over 100 officers and men. This completed, he was proceeding out of the canal, when he heard that an officer was in the water. He returned, rescued him, and then proceeded calmly as if engaged in a practice manoeuvre. Three men were shot down at his side whilst he conned his ship. On clearing the entrance to the canal, the steering gear broke down. He manoeuvred his boat by the engines, and avoided complete destruction by steering so close in under the Mole that the guns in the batteries could not depress sufficiently to fire on the boat. The whole of this operation was carried out under constant machine-gun fire at a few yards' range. It was solely due to this officer's courage and daring that *ML 282* succeeded in saving so many valuable lives. *LG 23 July 1918. A pre-war slate merchant and cotton spinner. He was MP for Blackburn, 1918-22. Died 20 March 1939, cremated at Golders Green Crematorium, London. VC in private ownership.*

FINCH, Norman Augustus Sergeant, Royal Marine Artillery

For most conspicuous gallantry. Sergeant Finch (regimental number 12150) was second in command of the pompoms and Lewis guns in the foretop of *Vindictive* under Lieutenant Charles N.B. Rigby, RMA. At one period, the *Vindictive* was being hit every few seconds, chiefly in the upper works, from which splinters caused many casualties. It was difficult to locate the guns which were doing most damage but Lieutenant Rigby, Sergeant Finch and the Marines in the foretop, kept up a continuous fire with pompoms and Lewis guns, changing rapidly from one target to another and thus keeping the enemy's fire down to some considerable extent.

Unfortunately, two heavy shells made direct hits on the foretop, which was completely exposed to enemy concentration of fire. All in the top were killed or disabled except Sergeant Finch, who was, however, severely wounded; nevertheless, he showed consummate bravery, remaining in this battered and exposed position. He once more got a Lewis gun into action, and kept up a continuous fire, harassing the enemy on the Mole, until the foretop received another direct hit, the remainder of the armament being then completely put out of action. Before the top was destroyed, Sergeant Finch had done invaluable work, and by his bravery undoubtedly saved many lives. *LG 19 July 1918.*

This very gallant sergeant of the Royal Marine Artillery was selected by the 4th Battalion of Royal Marines, to receive his Victoria Cross under Rule 13. During a radio interview, Sergeant N.A. Finch VC remarked 'This isn't really mine. I'm only selected to wear it on behalf of the regiment, and when I die it will have to be returned to the regiment.' *He died, aged 76, at Portsmouth on 15 March 1966. VC held by Brittania Royal Naval College, Dartmouth.*

HARRISON, Arthur Leyland Lieutenant Commander, Royal Navy

Posthumous award of the Victoria Cross. For most conspicuous gallantry at Zeebrugge on the night of 22/23 April 1918.

This officer was in command of the Naval Storming Parties embarked in *Vindictive*.

Immediately before coming alongside the Mole Lieutenant Commander Harrison was struck on the head by a fragment of shell, which broke his jaw and knocked him senseless. Recovering consciousness, he proceeded onto the Mole and took over command of his party, who were attacking the seaward end of the Mole. The silencing of the guns on the Mole head was of the first importance, and though in a position fully exposed to the enemy's machine-gun fire, Lieutenant Commander Harrison gathered his men together and led the attack. He was killed at the head of his men, all of whom were either killed or wounded.

Lieutenant Commander Harrison, though severely wounded, and undoubtedly in great pain, displayed indomitable resolution and courage of the highest order in pressing his attack, knowing as he did that any delay in silencing the guns might jeopardise the main object of the expedition i.e. the blocking of the Zeebrugge canal. *LG 17 March 1918. Born Torquay. He died, aged 32, on 23 April 1918. No known grave. VC held by Brittania Royal Naval College, Dartmouth.*

An artist's impression of the fight on the Mole close to where Lieutenant Commander Harrison won the Victoria Cross.

McKENZIE, Albert Edward Able Seaman, Royal Navy

For most conspicuous gallantry. This rating belonged to B Company a seaman storming party. On the night of the operation, he landed on the Mole with his machine gun in the face of great difficulties and did very good work, using his gun to the utmost advantage. He advanced down the Mole with Lieutenant Commander Harrison, who with most of his party was killed, and accounted for several of the enemy running from a shelter to a destroyer alongside the Mole. This very gallant seaman was severely wounded whilst working his gun in an exposed position. *LG* 19 July 1918.

Able Seaman McKenzie [O.N. J31736 [Ch]] was selected by the men of the *Vindictive*, *Iris II*, and *Daffodil* and of the naval assaulting force to receive the Victoria Cross under Rule 13. *After being shot in the back and the right foot, the twenty-year-old recovered from his wounds only to die of influenza on 3 November 1918. Interred Camberwell Cemetery, London. VC held by Imperial War Museum.*

A public welcome for Able Seaman Albert Edward McKenzie VC.

SANDFORD, Richard Douglas Lieutenant, Royal Navy

For conspicuous gallantry. This officer was in command of submarine *C3*, and most skilfully placed that vessel in between the piles of the viaduct before lighting his fuse and abandoning her. He eagerly undertook this hazardous enterprise, although well aware (as were all his crew) that if the means of rescue failed and he or any of the crew were in the water at the moment of the explosion, they would be killed outright by the force of such an explosion. Yet Sandford disdained to use the gyro steering, which would have enabled him and his crew to abandon the submarine at a safe distance, and preferred to make sure, as far as humanly possible, of the accomplishment of his duty. *LG* 23 July 1918. *He was the son of the Archdeacon of Exeter. The 27-year-old died on 23 November 1918 of typhoid fever in Cleveland Hospital, Grangetown, Yorkshire. VC held in Brittania Royal Naval College, Dartmouth.*

Breaching of the viaduct connecting the mole by submarine C3.

Victoria Cross awards for Ostend operation

BOURKE, Rowland Richard Louis Lieutenant, Royal Naval Volunteer Reserve

Volunteered for rescue work in command of *ML 276*, and followed *Vindictive* into Ostend, engaging the enemy's machine guns on both piers with Lewis guns. After *ML 254* had backed out, Lieutenant Bourke laid his vessel alongside *Vindictive* to make further search. Finding no one, he withdrew, but hearing cries in the water he again entered the harbour, and after a prolonged search eventually found Lieutenant Sir John Alleyane and two ratings all badly wounded in the water clinging to an upended skiff, and rescued them. During all the time the motor launch was under a heavy fire at close range, being hit in fifty-five places, once by a six-inch shell – two of her crew being killed and others wounded. The vessel was seriously damaged and speed greatly reduced. Lieutenant Bourke however managed to bring her out until he fell in with a Monitor, which took him in tow. This episode displayed daring and skill of a very high order, and Lieutenant Bourke's bravery and perseverance undoubtedly saved the lives of Lieutenant Alleyane and two of *Vindictive*'s crew. *LG* 28 August 1918.

He died, aged sixty-three, on 28 November 1958. Interred Royal Oak Burial Park, Victoria, Canada. VC held by National Archives of Canada, Ottawa.

CRUTCHLEY, Victor Alexander Charles DSC Lieutenant, Royal Navy

This officer was in *Brilliant* in the unsuccessful attempt to block Ostend on the night of 22/23 April, and at once volunteered for a further effort. He acted as first Lieutenant of *Vindictive*, and worked with untiring energy fitting out that ship for further service. On the night of 9/10 May, after his commanding officer had been killed and the second in command severely wounded, Lieutenant Crutchley took command of *Vindictive* and did his utmost by manoeuvring the engines to place that ship in an effective position. He displayed great bravery in both the *Vindictive* and *ML 254*, which rescued the crew after the charges had been blown and the former vessel sunk between the piers of Ostend harbour, and did not leave the *Vindictive* until he had made a thorough search with an electric torch for survivors under a very

136

heavy fire. Lieutenant Crutchley took command of *ML 254* when the commanding officer sank exhausted from his wounds, the second in command having been killed. The vessel was full of wounded and very seriously damaged by shellfire, the fore part being flooded. With indomitable energy and by dint of baling with buckets and shifting weight aft, Lieutenant Crutchley and the unwounded kept her afloat, but the leaks could not be kept under, and she was in a sinking condition, with her forecastle nearly awash, when picked up by HMS *Warwick*. The bearing of this very gallant officer and fine seaman throughout these operations off the Belgian coast was altogether admirable and an inspiring example to all thrown in contact with him. *LG* 28 August 1918. *He died 24 January 1986, aged 93. VC in private ownership.*

Lieutenant Crutchley DSC searching for survivors.

DRUMMOND, Geoffrey Heneage Lieutenant, Royal Naval Volunteer Reserve

Volunteered for rescue work in command of *ML 254*. Following *Vindictive* to Ostend, when off the piers a shell burst on board, killing Lieutenant Gordon Ross and Deckhand J. Thomas, wounding the coxswain, and severely wounding Lieutenant Drummond in three places. Notwithstanding his wounds, he remained on the bridge, navigated his vessel, already seriously damaged by shellfire, into Ostend harbour, placed her alongside *Vindictive* and took off two officers and thirty-eight men, some of whom were killed and many wounded while embarking. When informed there was no one alive left on board he backed his vessel clear of the piers before sinking exhausted from his wounds. When HMS *Warwick* fell in with *ML 254* off Ostend half an hour later the latter was in sinking condition. It was due to the indomitable courage of this very gallant officer that the majority of the crew of the *Vindictive* were

Motor Launch *254* rescuing the crew of the *Vindictive* at Ostend.

renumed *LG* 20 August 1918.

During the Second World War, he served as a Lieutenant Commander in the Royal Naval Patrol Service. He died aged 55 on 21 April 1941, at Rotherhithe. London. VC in private ownership.

During the aftermath of the raids Keyes became involved in a war of words with the Admiralty, who took issue with the number of Victoria Crosses he recommended. It argued decorations were awarded on a ratio of the numbers involved with a certain amount being allotted to the lower decks, his proportion of officers being too high. Keyes argued that due to the number of small boats used in the operation, with almost as many officers as men on board, the fixed guidelines were unworkable. Eventually, under pressure from Keyes and with the King's intervention, they accepted Keyes' recommendations.

A plethora of other gallantry awards for the actions followed, making it almost possible to comprehend the horrors of the nocturnal raids simply by reading the *London Gazette* citations. The awards for the attacks on 22/23 April 1918 appeared in the 23 July 1918 *London Gazette*.

Where every moment had its deed and every deed its hero was reflected in the initial award of six VCs (rising to eight with the posthumas awards

A 20 April 1923 memorandum from Brigade Major H. C. Pope, Brigade Major Chatham Barracks. This requests Bugler Forrester to return his service certificate so it may be endorsed that he participated in the ballot for the Victoria Cross.

D. 308a. (Established — snuary, 1603.)

MEMORANDUM.

From The Brigade Major,

R.M. Barracks, Chatham.

20th April, 1923.

To *Mr (W Forrester / 8 .... no Road / Liverpool, Lancs.*

No. S/1788x

In order that your Service Certificate may be endorsed to the effect that you participated in the ballot for the award of the Victoria Cross granted for the operation against Zeebrugge, please forward your Certificate to me in enclosed stamped addressed envelope

H C Pope,
Brigade Major.

139

to Bradford and Harrison, LG 17 April 1919). Four Companions of the Bath (CB), two Companions of St Michael and St George (CMG), twenty Distinguished Service Orders (DSO), one bar to DSO, twenty-eight Distinguished Service Crosses (DSC), two bars to DSC, sixteen Conspicuous Gallantry Medals (CGM). Twenty-two Distinguished Service Medals (DSM) went to men from *Vindictive*, eight to *Thetis*, nine to *Iphigenia*, eight to *Intrepid*, five to *Brilliant*, six to *Sirius*, four to *Iris* and four to *Daffodil*. Three medals each went to men of *Phoebe* and *North Star* and one to Yeoman Signaller Elliot on board *Warwick*. The Picket Boats', Motor Launches' and Coastal Boats' crews received thirty-one awards. Three bars to the DSM were also awarded.

The seamen storming parties' role was acknowledged by ten DSMs to A company, seven to B company, five to C company, five to D company. The Royal Marines received thirteen awards; two of these were to the RMA detachment. The Mentions In Despatches [MID] numbered 278.

The honours for the lesser 9/10th May Ostend raid appeared in the 28 August *London Gazette*. They comprised three VCs, one CB, one CMG, seven DSOs, three bars to DSO, nine DSCs, two bars to DSC, two CGMs, sixty-four DSMs and fifty-eight MIDs. Following the raids, over fifty men received immediate promotion due to their gallantry and leadership qualities.

Medal presentation by King George. Keyes is on the left, a grinning Beatty is on the right.

Chapter Eight

CEMETERIES AND MEMORIALS

By the very nature of naval warfare, the fatalities are often denied a known final resting place. The marines and seamen killed during the raids were no exception; when their bodies plunged into the North Sea they were at the mercy of the tidal current. The sea does not always give up its dead; however, in the aftermath of the raids numerous British corpses were recovered from the sea. The Germans interred the dead with full military honours in the nearest churchyard to the recovery point. The fallen raiders lie in four Belgian cemeteries and one in the Netherlands.

In this region, British First World War deaths are significantly less than those of the Second World War. The BEF was involved here during the later stages of the defence of Belgium following the German invasion in May 1940 and suffered many casualties during the withdrawal to Dunkirk. Commonwealth forces returned in September 1944 (the Canadians liberated Oostende on 8 September 1944); many airmen were shot down or crashed during flying operations in the intervening years.

When visiting any of the cemeteries please ensure you sign the visitors' register, these are contained inside a small box usually sited near the entrance or an accessible cemetery structure.

Blankenberge Town Cemetery

As its name suggests, this is the final resting place of the local community; the cemetery also contains two CWGC plots, the larger being the Second World War plot containing eighty burials, fourteen of which are unidentified. Over half the graves belong to RAF personnel lost when *HMLST 420* sank off Ostend on 7 November 1944, others were shot down or crashed over Belgium. To the left of the main gate a small plot holds ten First World War burials, including four killed on 23 April 1918. This is a serene and almost intimate plot, for we understand why the *North Star* men and VC winner Lieutenant Commander George Bradford lie here. This cemetery is not an open site and access is limited to normal cemetery hours.

Cement House Cemetery, Langemarke

This village was in German possession from April 1915 to August 1917 and from April to September 1918. Considering the enemy occupied the village at the time of the raid and its distance from the sea it seems an unlikely place for the interment of a Zeebrugge marine. CH/14455

Private T. Sneyd RMLI, who died on St. George's Day, lies here in grave XX. A. 26. Originally posted as missing he was either killed or died of wounds. Following enquiries with the CWGC office, the reason for this grave location became apparent. In 1922 and subsequent years some 500 French graves were removed; since then, the vacated spaces have been used for graves brought in from communal cemeteries and churchyards in the area when their maintenance could no longer be assured. Originally Private Sneyd and nine other First World War casualties lay within Heist-sur-Mer Communal Cemetery (the coastal town of Heist lies a few kilometres east of Zeebrugge). On 9 March 1966 their remains were re-interred in Cement House Cemetery, named after the fortified farm building on the Langemark-Boesinghe [now Boezinge] road. The cemetery is located in Langemark north of Ypres [Ieper] off the N313. From the Markt take the Korte leperstraat, at the end turn right into Boezingsraat, past the first turning on the left and the cemetery is 100 metres on the left hand side. There are now 3,576 Commonwealth Great War servicemen buried or commemorated here; 2,408 are unidentified. The cemetery continues to be used for the burial of remains that continue to be discovered.

Flushing [Vlissen] Northern Cemetery, Netherlands
This cemetery lies beyond our tour area as it is approximately twenty-eight kilometres as the crow flies east of Zeebrugge. The port of Flushing is on the south coast of Walcheren in the Schelde Estuary. In the Great War Plot are buried men drowned at sea, among them sailors of HMS *Tornado*, sunk just before Christmas 1917, two men killed at Zeebrugge and airmen killed over the North Sea. There are thirty-six Commonwealth Great War interments, eleven of whom are unidentified. The following Zeebrugge raiders lie here: Leading Seaman Ernest Edward Henniker HMS *North Star*, Private Ernest Ainger Batt and Private D. O'Sullivan, both RMLI of the depot ship HMS *Hindustan*, also Deck Hand Joseph Edward Baxter RNR killed on *ML 424*. A memorial in Belgian petit granite stands at the back of the plot. The Belgian society 'Herdenken om te Strijden' erected this memorial of a woman in Zeeland costume bending over a dying soldier. The plot and memorial are situated close to the main entrance. There are also 200 Second World War allied casualties interred here.

Oostende New Communal Cemetery
This is the largest cemetery we shall visit in West-Vlaanderen. 366 World War Two personnel lie here in a plot, adjoining the graves of fifty from the Great War, including eleven from Operation ZO. The traveller should

note there are two major cemeteries in Oostende, a considerable distance apart; ensure you visit the new cemetery *not* the old one near the beach.

Zeebrugge Churchyard

Near the anniversary of the raid, a well attended memorial ceremony in Flemish and English is conducted in Sint Donaas church, culminating in a wreath laying ceremony within the adjoining cemetery. Bounded by a low brick wall, the entrance is through an archway; notice the German inscription above. This is an official German military cemetery containing 173 of their war dead.

Contemporary photographs reveal the site's origins as a scruffy plot far removed from the orderly, nicely maintained cemetery of today. A total of thirty empire servicemen are buried here, only seventeen are identified but a special memorial commemorates an RNAS officer known to be buried amongst them. Fixed to the wall is the smallest CWGC memorial to the missing, dedicated to the memory of three officers and an eighteen-year-old mechanic killed on the Mole and who have no known grave. They are Wing Commander Brock, Lieutenant Commander Harrison VC, Lieutenant Hawkins and Mechanic J. Rouse, a young Birmingham volunteer who previously served on HMS *Myncs*.

A close-up of the now missing memorial:
3 English Officers
7 English Marines
2 English Sailors
2 English Stokers

A German-provided headstone in Zeebrugge cemetery marking the Zeebrugge British dead.

In the centre of two rows of Portland stone headstones stands the Salvage Corps memorial, whose eroded inscription reads, 'To the memory of those who fell in this place on St. George's Day 23 April 1918. Erected by members of the British Salvage Section, St. George's Day 1920.' The cross and main body of the memorial have reduced in height since its dedication, possibly due to war damage. The memorials within this cemetery have altered over the years, judging from contemporary photographs and postcards. A tall German memorial once stood in front of the transept; this is long gone. Possibly where the Salvage Corps Memorial now stands a German burial cross engraved with the numbers of the British graves stood. As it was removed in April 1920 at the time of the Salvage Corps dedication this seems the most likely explanation for its absence.

Respecting Valour Memorials

In recent times, as part of their Respecting Valour campaign, serving and former Royal Marines have financed small Italian marble memorials to commemorate their Victoria Cross winners, in this instance Sergeant Finch and Captain Bamford. Their memorials are sited in Zeebrugge churchyard along the right hand wall and are the only ones located in the vicinity where the Royal Marine recipient fought.

Vindictive Memorial [Oostende]

On 16 August 1920, a civilian contractor raised the wreck of *Vindictive* off the seabed but five years elapsed before the old warhorse was completely dismantled. Several locals assured the author that the breaker became insolvent due to the salvage difficulties encountered in this task. Somebody had the foresight to secure a section of the vessel's bow as a permanent memorial to the raids. As *Vindictive* fought in both raids, it is a very appropriate choice of memorial, formerly visited each St. George's Day for over fifty years by veterans of the Zeebrugge Association. A transverse bulkhead proudly proclaims 'In Memoriam 23-IV-1918, 10-V-1918'. There are also two wooden masts of doubtful vintage from *Intrepid* and *Thetis*. In a 1990 edition of *Before Endeavours Fade* the author, Rose Coombes MBE, states: 'The upper sections of the mast of HMS *Thetis* (nearest the road) is fairly new as the original fell to pieces with wood rot. (I know for I gave a section of it to the Imperial War Museum, London!)' Since she took her photograph of the bow section, a component has disappeared off the deck on the port side, aft of the name.

Zeebrugge Memorial

This memorial is really a collection of memorials, each one having its

144

own individual tale. Within a few hundred metres once stood the original Zeebrugge Memorial, officially unveiled on the seventh anniversary of the raid by King Albert, the Belgian sovereign. Keyes, Carpenter, veterans, many officers and 250 sailors attended the ceremony. The memorial, a seventy feet high stone column surmounted by a bronze statue of St. George slaying the dragon, also bore Sir Roger Keyes', signal 'St. George for England'. Below, a main inscription read, 'In memory of St. George's day, 1918 when every moment had its deed and every deed its hero'. During 1942 the occupying Germans destroyed the monument and melted down the bronze statue.

On 23 April 1983 the dedication of a replacement memorial took place; this new memorial depicted a relief map of the raid. Directly in front of

Remembering Valour memorials. The two proud Royal Marines are on the left; Warrant Officer II Mick Plater, the Royal Marines' historian. On the right is Sergeant Mark Allen.

the monument several stone tablets bearing ships' names from the original memorial were embedded into the pavement. Due to port expansion,

145

The original Zeebrugge Memorial unveiled by King Albert of the Belgians on 23 April 1925.
The plaque that once marked the position of *Vindictive*.

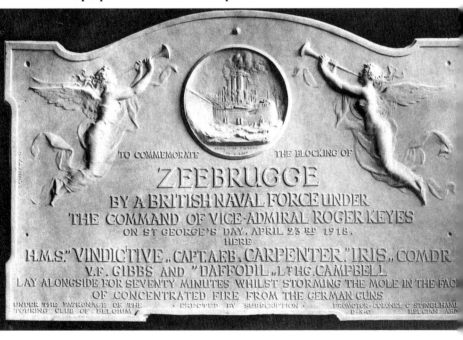

TO COMMEMORATE   THE BLOCKING OF

ZEEBRUGGE
BY A BRITISH NAVAL FORCE UNDER
THE COMMAND OF VICE-ADMIRAL ROGER KEYES
ON ST GEORGE'S DAY, APRIL 23RD 1918.
HERE
H.M.S. "VINDICTIVE" CAPT. A.F.B. CARPENTER. "IRIS" COMDR
V.F. GIBBS AND "DAFFODIL" LT H.G. CAMPBELL
LAY ALONGSIDE FOR SEVENTY MINUTES WHILST STORMING THE MOLE IN THE FACE
OF CONCENTRATED FIRE FROM THE GERMAN GUNS
UNDER THE PATRONAGE OF THE   · ERECTED BY SUBSCRIPTION ·   PROMOTOR: COLONEL C. STINGLHAMBER
TOURING CLUB OF BELGIUM /   D.S.O.   BELGIAN ARMY

The original *C3* memorial, once sited on the Mole near the viaduct.

the memorial was relocated to its present site; at the same time several other memorials were located here. On the opposite page, a bronze tablet commemorates *Vindictive*, *Iris* and *Daffodil*. This once marked the

147

position where the three vessels lay alongside the Mole. Created by the medallist A. Bonnetain, the tablet was unveiled on 27 June 1926, by Prince Charles Theodore of Belgium. The tablet dedicated to *C3* is the work of the sculptor Pierre de Soete. The smoke produced by the great explosion liberates a female figure symbolising Great Britain. With a noble gesture, she indicates the road back towards England and with the other hand presents the VC to Lieutenant Sandford. This tablet and the dedicated stone memorial once marked where *C3* exploded. A small replacement cast plaque dedicated to 4th Battalion Royal Marines light infantry was unveiled in 1993.

Zeebrugge Memorial, Antwerp
There is a memorial to Lieutenant Commander Harrison, VC in the city of Antwerp.

A vintage scale model of a memorial dedicated to the blockship crews.

148

Chapter Nine

TOURS AND WALKS IN THE AREA

Tour One. Zeebrugge

The overnight sea cruise from Hull takes approximately twelve hours and arrives at Zeebrugge around 8.30 a.m. Passengers generally gather on deck to view the vessel entering harbour and it is doubtful if any of them are aware of the action fought here in 1918. In order to view the approaching Mole extension, the reader should take up a suitable vantage point on the starboard side of the ship (on the right hand side of the ship when looking forward). As the ferry cautiously approaches the harbour a low promontory surmounted by a lighthouse becomes discernible through the early morning mist, this is the last remaining section of the infamous Mole. Once guarded by its own battery of guns, it is not diffi-cult to understand the threat this breakwater posed to the block ships; indeed it makes all the more appreciable the colossal task faced by the marine and naval storming parties. The Mole extension halts abruptly where the two huge, light coloured, marine gas oil tanks are. Adjacent to the lighthouse, at right angles to the main channel, Captain Fryatt's SS *Brussels*, scuttled by the retreating Germans, lay until her salvage on 4

The Mole extension today on a misty St Georges Day morning.

The Mole today. In 1918 the cruiser and ferries passed to the right of the Mole.

August 1919. After reconditioning, her owners, the Great Eastern Railway, sold her in 1920. Her new owners named her *Lady Brussels*; she sailed on the Liverpool to Dublin service.

To the right of the Mole lies a network of interlocking concrete blocks, part of the Albert Dock II reclamation, bounded by a modern seawall. Using the Mole extension as a landmark, you should be able to visualise

St. George's Wanderling and the Zeebrugge memorial.

The current Zeebrugge memorial.

the vast concrete arc of the Mole demolished in the nineteen-eighties. The *Vindictive* steamed over the present site of the concrete blocks then berthed on the outer face of the breakwater (now reclaimed land) approximately several hundred yards seaward of the P & O buildings. The site where frenetic fighting occurred on that April night has disappeared beneath a sprawling, concrete container marshalling area. The ferry moors here, allowing a brief opportunity to contemplate the site of the diversionary raid. Finally, the extremity of the boom barrage protecting the inner harbour lay anchored at a point just inland of the outer gas oil tanks.

By crossing to the port side we have a panoramic view of the harbour; beyond this look for a red and white painted hoop steel tower, you will see the red brick of Saint Bridget's church tower visible above the third block of apartments, a church we later visit. The harbour has altered dramatically; since the modernisation of the port much of what we see did not exist in 1918. However, the harbour has evolved around the old channel. We need to disembark to see the other sights. Any visitors making this tour overland, possibly from the Ypres or the Calais direction, should follow the road signs for the Zeebrugge ferry terminal to join us at the first memorial, more or less outside the terminal complex.

Once clear of the terminal remember to drive on the right hand side of the road. Travel a very short distance along Leopold II Dam, look towards your right for a tall corner building, formerly the Residents Palace hotel. Beyond this on your left, the underground entrance to Zeebrugge Strand

151

The *C3* memorial now incorporated on the main memorial.

station is visible, a legacy of the railway network once serving the Mole; park in the small car park. Proceed to the tall building; a pleasant seaside pathway named Sint Georges Wanderling is directly in front and the concrete edifice on your right (possibly flanked with a Belgian and British flag) is the Zeebrugge Memorial, appropriately sited at the landward end of the former Mole. You are also within a stone's throw of the site of the six-inch gun '*Lubeck*' battery. As you gaze at children playing football

The Second World War memorial to the 19th Manitoba Dragoons.

along the broad pavement, it is difficult to imagine the events that occurred near here all those years ago. After a pause for contemplation, we leave for the next site.

Return to your car and, leaving the terminal behind, turn left at the traffic lights onto Kustlaan (N34) heading for the town of Zeebrugge. When you see a grey painted girder bridge across the Zeesluis canal, pull in on your right. Across the road, you should see an attractive memorial to the 19th Manitoba Dragoons, commemorating their action here on 3 November 1944.

The site has more significance to us as this is the Bruges canal lock gate. Had *Thetis* or *Intrepid* rammed this caisson the raid would have achieved its aims. With your back to the bridge, walk along Zeegeulstraat (the towpath bounding the dock) as far as you can. When looking seaward, look just beyond the point where the canal widens out, this is approximately where *Iphigenia* and *Intrepid* scuttled. To the left roughly mid way along the container quay (this is a modern construction), *Thetis*, with her fouled propellers, stranded herself. On the inland side of the canal bridge, when looking in the terminal direction, the road running parallel to, Zeesluis is Kapitan Fryatt Straat, named after the executed sea

153

The lock gate to the Bruges canal, the unachieved objective for *Thetis*.

captain, who also has a memorial in Bruges.

On returning to the car carry on in the same direction to Sint Donnas Kerk or Saint Donnas' church (follow the route of the tram-lines), this is approximately a kilometre away on your right. Look for an ornate red brick church with a slate roof. At the church, turn right into Sint Donnas Kerk Straat, then park. Walk past the church main door and a modern looking Belgian war memorial; you will then see a small cemetery, containing German and British war dead, enclosed by a red brick wall. Access is through the gates in the archway.

Immediately on the left, it is impossible to miss the communal grave of the German seamen from the torpedo boat destroyers *S15* and *S20*; the visitor may appreciate this brief explanation. In 1916 both vessels fought at

St Donnas' Church, Zeebrugge. A German war cemetery is next to the church. Eight Germans interred here died on St. George's Day; they lie here with their British adversaries killed in the same action.

154

Jutland as part of the VII Torpedo Flotilla. Their luck did not last for, on 5 June 1917, while off the Flanders coast, the Harwich Force intercepted *S20*. She was subsequently sunk by gunfire from the light cruiser *Centaur*. Forty-nine of her seventy-four man crew died; the recovered bodies lie here. This comrades' grave also records those killed on board *S15* due to a mine explosion on 21 August 1917. The vessel was so severely damaged, despite a towage to port, she went to the Ghent breakers.

Towards the right of the 'Salvage' cross lay eight unidentified Zeebrugge raiders, known only to God. On the left only Charles Phelps Tuckey RMLI is identified, two officers and three marines killed on the raid are unknown. Another raider, twenty-two-year-old Devon man Corporal George Arthur Osborne RMLI, also lies here, as does Petty Officer John Albert Mayers. The six unknown marines are a puzzle as 'With Full and Grateful Hearts', the register of Royal Marine deaths in the Great War states that only James Colligan and Thomas Moore have no known graves. The fact that only three of the raiders here are identified offers some insight into the ferocity of the engagement fought here, where the next of kin were denied the slender comfort of at least knowing the final resting place of their loved ones.

Upon leaving the visitor may notice far away to the right *Westhinder II*, a 1950s red painted lightship; next to her, in the Visserhaven dock, you will find a Foxtrot Type 641 Russian submarine *U-480*. As the 100 metre long vessel is open to the public, she may be of interest to naval historians. Visitors can either walk from the church or return to your car and rejoin the Kustlaan and head for the light ship; before you reach this on the opposite side of the carriageway you will see an entrance. Park here

Visitor attraction: Foxtrot Type 641 Russian submarine U-480.

The original Salvage Corps memorial and Zeebrugge fallen.

The Salvage Corps memorial and graves today.

The Zeebrugge memorial to the missing.

The graves of four unidentified marines, two unknown seamen and two Stokers, all killed on 23 April 1918. The Zeebrugge Memorial is on the extreme right.

or in Vissersstraat [a side street]. Both vessels are part of the 'Seafront Zeebrugge' marine theme park, housed in three halls formerly used by the fishing industry. The entrance is at the furthest hall, but this does give an opportunity to stroll up Vissersstraat, where there are numerous pavement cafés specialising in fresh seafood. If you are a little squeamish, at the end of the road there is a car park; facing this you will find a pleasant café offering excellent lasagne etc.

Until the modernisation of the port, the town had a museum housed in the basement of the Palace Hotel; when this faced demolition the St. George's Day exhibits went to Bruges. The collection reputedly contained steel sections of the ships, uniforms and assorted artefacts from the raids. Due to inadequate storage facilities, the larger artefacts allegedly deteriorated to such a state that they were scrapped. The Bruges archives do contain a modest collection but an appointment is required to view. My enquiries at 'Seafront Zeebrugge' revealed that they did have a Zeebrugge Raid section, so with great anticipation I set off in search of the display, only to be severely disappointed. Here you will find a lacklustre collection of poor photocopies displayed in gloomy surroundings.

The Zeebrugge museum, which no longer exists.

On a mute television black and white Imperial War Museum film flickers, while in the background a taped recording of the history of the fishing fleet overpowers the display. There are three items possibly of Great War origins, the first being a cloth wall hanging depicting L'Attaque de Zeebrugge; situated below this, on two wooden trestles, lies a timber framed relief map of the attack. Both these artefacts bear a great resemblance to the central panel of the Zeebrugge memorial. As these lack labels, one can only ponder if these were the inspiration for the memorial's design. Above the doorway there is an embroidery of the famous signal and reply reading 'Saint George for England! May we give the Dragon's tail a damned good twist'. In the Belgian navy section, amongst other weaponry, there is a First World War German torpedo. In the dock, you can explore U-480 and wonder how 75 men existed in the claustrophobic confines of this 1960s diesel electric submarine.

Once back in the car you may wish to drive around to Admiral Keyes Plein,where the area resembles an English village green enclosed by a low hedge. Look for the flag pylon (likely flying national flags) either side of the three rectangular blocks placed in an inverted T, approximately eight foot high. When contractors demolished the Mole during the port extensions, these blocks were retained to form a memorial. On each anniversary of the raid a well attended remembrance ceremony occurs here to commemorate the legend of St. George's Day. Please consult the map for directions.

While replacing the roof upon the local police station, items recalling the raid were discovered, including copies of postcards as used in this book, sketches of personalities, and a canvas painting of the Zeebrugge Association 1918 badge. This comprises a white ensign superimposed by a golden dragon with a twisted tail. However, the star attraction is a frame containing four items from *C3*, three of which are accompanied by scraps of paper with hand written provenance. An old strapless wristwatch was used for setting the timer on *C3*. An accompanying bunch of keys contains the very key used to wind up the time delay mechanism. Another small cross-shaped object is unidentified but required replacement due to damage. A fourth item is unidentified. Please note that these are contained upstairs in a working police station and are not on public display.

Four items from *C3*.

The estimated time for visiting the memorials and cemetery would be two hours. This excludes lunch or visiting 'Seafront Zeebrugge'.

Tour Two. Blankenberge See map

Retrace your route along the Kustlaan (N34), heading in the direction of Ostend; this small city is now named Oostende. The seaside town of Blankenberge is approximately four kilometres west from the ferry terminal and twenty kilometres east of Oostende. The N34 is a coastal dual carriageway shared with trams; throughout the journey the sand dunes should be on your right hand. These dunes and salt marshes were heavily fortified during both world wars; almost all traces of the fortifications have now disappeared. Along this stretch of road lies the Dallas Campsite, offering 150 touring caravan pitches.

The N34 Koning Albertlaan leads directly to the town square (by the station). The cemetery is located via Kerkstraat, N371 and then turn right onto Zuidlaan for 500 metres, finally turning left along Landijk for 100 metres to the cemetery. If this appears daunting, from the square follow the road to the left. Turn right at the traffic lights then left into Kdeswert Laan; the cemetery is straight ahead. A high brick wall flanks the cemetery gates, with parking bays either side.

When looking along the central roadway in the distance you will notice the Cross of Sacrifice of the 1939-45 plot; the cemetery register is located here. The Great War section, containing ten Commonwealth burials, is

The First World War section of Blankenberge cemetery.

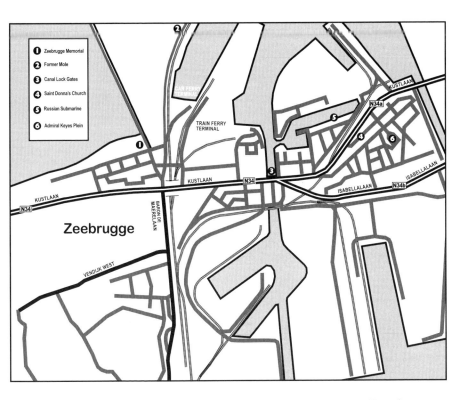

Map legend:

❶ Zeebrugge Memorial
❷ Former Mole
❸ Canal Lock Gates
❹ Saint Donna's Church
❺ Russian Submarine
❻ Admiral Keyes Plein

Zeebrugge

visible from the gateway. Look over to your left, by the small office, for two neat rows of white headstones.

The graves contain two unidentified seamen unconnected with the raid and four Commonwealth aviators including two from 204 RAF Squadron killed on the same day. Of the four raid casualties lying here, Lieutenant Commander G. N. Bradford VC has the greatest claim to fame. While attempting to secure *Iris* to the Mole he bravely climbed onto the parapet; cut down by machine-gun bullets he fell into the sea. After several days, his body was washed up on the beach. The Germans buried him here with full military honours.

He and three of his brothers were the pride of Darlington, for between them they earned two Victoria Crosses, a DSO, two MCs and three MIDs. Roland Boys Bradford VC, MC made the ultimate sacrifice in 1917. A fourth brother had an undistinguished military career. The eldest brother, Thomas A. Bradford DSO, survived the war.

Two seamen and a mechanic from *North Star* also lie here. To visit both plots in this cemetery allow approximately forty minutes.

Tour Three. Oostende (Ostend)

We now rejoin the N34 and head for Oostende, preferably avoiding the weekend traffic. On the way you will see amongst the dunes signs for Domane Raversijde, a popular tourist attraction. For a modest fee, you can see part of Hitler's West Wall, there is also a folk museum and café/restaurant. As you approach the town you drive along the Dokter Eduard Moreauxlaan; this will take you over several harbour bridges and the railway. At the small roundabout go straight ahead onto Ringlaan, leading to President Kennedy Plein, a large roundabout; take the turning for the R31 Elisabethlaan. Carry on until you see a church and a round-about; Stuiverstraat will be on your left and connects with the roundabout. The cemetery is located 800 metres along the Stuiverstraat on the right hand side of the road.

Once through the gates the pristine CWGC plot is immediately recognisable; our focus of attention lies close to the Cross of Sacrifice, where an arc of headstones are. Ten men from Operation ZO lie here, including Able Seamen G. Hillier and R.P. Payne from *North Star* and an unknown seaman, all killed on St. George's Day. The remaining seven died during the second Ostend operation, on board *Vindictive*. Two men prominent in our narrative rest here, namely Commander Godsal DSO, struck down by the blast of shell and also the tall, good-looking eighteen-year-old Lieutenant Angus Hope MacLachlan, whose kitbag mysteriously found its own way onto *Vindictive*. Two years previous, he fought at Jutland on the Bellerophon class battleship *Temeraire*. His heartbroken parents placed this epitaph on his headstone: 'In such a death there is no sting, in

The Great War section of Oostende New Communal Cemetery.

Oostende

A Oostende New Cemetery
B Belgian War Memorial WW1 & WW2
C Diarmuid Memorial
D Railway Station
E Channel Ferry Quay
F Bow Section of Vindictive
G Fort Napoleon WW1 Gun position
H Position of Vindictive 1918 to 1925

Maria Hendrikapark

Verenigde Natieslaan

President Kennedy Plein

Ringlaan

Elisabethlaan

Leopold III-laan

Torhoutsesteenweg

such a grave everlasting victory'.

The monitors involved in the raids are rarely mentioned, for they fulfilled an unglamorous yet vital role. During the Ostend bombardment, they threw caution to the wind and approached closer to the shore than usual. While under fire from the coastal batteries they sustained casualties: one representative from each *Marshal Soult, Prince Eugene, Sir John Moore* and *Erubus* originally posted as missing, lie here reminding us of their participation.

Among the adjoining rows of headstones, the observant may notice a headstone without an engraved unit badge, belonging to S. Cameron, a Salvage Shipwright killed on RFA *Hughli* on 26 April 1919. The war reparation vessel, formerly *Valencia* of the Hamburg-Amerika [sic] Line, may have struck an uncharted mine, as five of her crew lie here. She was salved off Ostend in October 1919 the renamed *Tinhow,* she was torpedoed and sunk in 1943. The maximum time required for this visit would be one hour.

Retrace your route back to the President Kennedy Plein roundabout and follow any signage indicating the station, ferry terminal, *Mercator* or jachthaven. The former fishing dock is now a haven for luxury yachts and the white sailing ship *Mercator*; find a suitable parking space near this. The parking meters accept euros, allow for a stay of at least two hours'

An unflattering view of the memorial to the raid's heroes.

duration. It is far easier to complete this final tour on foot; the walk to the bow of *Vindictive* will take about ten minutes.

Using the station as a starting point, walk away from the dock in the direction of the bus and tram terminus; you may feel you are heading in the wrong direction but continue heading for the ornate road bridge. On your left, you will see an employees' car park and at the base of the bridge on the right, there are steps: go up these. Turn left and cross the bridge, head towards the iron girder bridge across the canal; before you reach, this in a sunken, lawned area, you will see the grey paintwork of *Vindictive*. Take the road running parallel to the canal where you will see steps down to the memorial and canal side. Should they be locked a gate on the opposite side of the canal is generally open for workers. Cross by the next canal bridge; the detached property on the left relates to the harbour board: out of courtesy, I requested permission here. Visitors then have to make a precarious crossing over the lock gate; it is well worth the effort. Words fail to express how it feels to touch such a huge, illustrious part of Great War history, few such relics now lie in Flanders fields. On close examination, the indents in her hull caused by shellfire are visible. A marine propeller once occupied the space between the mast of *Intrepid* [nearest the bow] and *Iphigenia*; phosphor bronze is a valuable scrap metal and perhaps this explains the propeller's fate. The Demey locks link the old commercial docks with the outer harbour channel. This area may once have been a hive of industry for Belgian seafarers and enemy shipping but it is now an almost deserted location.

The 109-year-old section of *Vindictive* proudly stands sentinel over the outlet she courageously failed to block, a monument to the gallant men slain upon her decks.

Now walk back to the station; you may notice the road along the right hand side of the yacht haven is Vindictivelaan or Vindictive Lane. Within this quaint network of docks, elegant sailing ships and fishing smacks once moored. Under German occupation the naval base and, inadvertently, its civilian areas were routinely bombed. Cross over to the Iceland fishing vessel *Amandine*, turn right and walk up Visserskaai in the direction of the piers. Along from the boat you will see a sign for St. Peter und Paul Kirche, next to this you will find a two-section concrete memorial to Belgian service personnel killed in two World Wars. Then rejoin the coastal roadway; there are numerous restaurants and even an Irish themed 'Molly Malone's' along this route. On the high ground across the docks you should see Fort Napoleon, which was used as a casino by the Germans; near this ancient fortification the four eleven inch guns of the German *Hindenburg* Battery once bombarded the block ships.

As the dock system gives way to glorious sandy beaches, two long

One of the pier's at Oostende.

The same pier in 1913.

piers reach out; the nearest, west pier (Westerstaketsel), was constructed in 1887. It is a considerable walk along the planked decking to the café near its extreme tip, but the thirsty tourist may savour a refreshing drink at this point. More or less opposite here *Vindictive* lay alongside the Oosterstaketsellay (east pier) until she was broken up. Given the surface area of the North Sea, it now becomes understandable why Commander Godsal encountered such difficulty locating this entrance.

As you walk back towards the beach to the right you will see, sited on the Zeehelden Plein, a tall column surmounted by a sailor, a memorial to Belgian seamen. Continue walking along the pleasant promenade for about fifteen minutes. Near the Royal Gallery you will see the Beach House Surf Club. The Gneisenau Battery of four inch guns once stood near here. This concludes our tour.

The Belgians fought fiercely in this sector during two World Wars. This face of the memorial commemorates the fallen of the Great War.

The Belgian memorial to seamen built on the old semaphore site.

The night was dark with fitful showers
On Zeebrugge's sandy coast,
No light shone from the hidden forts
Where lurked the Teuton host.
The Mole stretched out its giant arm
As if to bridge the main
And only sounds of breaking foam
Came amidst the falling rain.
But then from out the murky gloom
A phantom form appeared
With lengthy hull and funnels tall,
Down on the Mole she steered
And with her two of lesser size
Stole forth in grim array.
While other shapes crept slowly towards
The dark, forbidding bay.
Bold Keyes contrived with martial skill
No blow of his should fail
He vowed that on St. George's Day
He'd 'twist the dragon's tail!'
So on the *Warwick*'s narrow deck
He waited for the hour,
To harry Shroeder's pirate nest
With the might of Britain's power.
The fickle wind rolled swiftly back
The curtain thick of smoke
And then the Germans knew their fate
And every cannon spoke.
Lights flashed on high on every side,
And glanced across the sea.
While thunders rolled in anger deep
Adown the shore and lea,
And distant guns joined in the song
That shook the sea and sky.
And midst their sound there rang aloud
Old England's battle cry!
The fire balls flew like emerald stars
And bullets fell like snow
But our marines had one reply,
'Now over boys you go'.
The Mole was gained, the stormers passed
Across that bridge of hell

As still the old Vindictives
Their tale of carnage tell.
Brave Elliot fell, and Halahan,
And Brock and many more
But nothing checked those heroes left,
Who swept the pier and shore;
And while they held the foe at bay,
In bomb and bayonet fray,
The blocking cruisers gained their goal,
And barred the channel way!
Then with a parting salvo sent
By every British crew,
Vindictive's smoking, belching fire,
Stood out to sea anew,
And in the darkness of the night,
Was lost as but a speck
But Carpenter had left his mark
Of slaughter, flame and wreck!

Oh England, mourn thy gallant sons,
Marines and sailors, too
Who died like paladins of old,
To King and Country true.
But dry thy tears for every age
Their glory shall extol:
So when you hail St. George's Day
Remember Zeebrugge Mole.

Published in the *Globe and Laurel* July 1918.

BIBLIOGRAPHY

Before Endeavours Fade. Rose Coombes, MBE. Battle of Britain Prints International Ltd., Church St, London. 1990.

Blocking of Zeebrugge, The. Capt. Alfred F.B. Carpenter, VC RN. Mayflower Press, Plymouth. 1926.

Britain's sea soldiers – A history of the Royal Marines 1914–19. General Sir H.E. Blumberg KCB RN. Swiss & Co., 1927.

Business in Great Waters. John Terraine. Leo Cooper Ltd. 1989.

Distinguished Service Medal 1914–1920, The. W.H. Fevyer. J.B. Hayward & Son. Polstead, Suffolk. 1982.

From Trench and Turret. Royal Marine letters and diaries 1914–18. S.M. Holloway. Royal Marines Museum. Holbrook & Son, Portsmouth.

Globe and Laurel, The. July 1918.

History of the War. Vol. XVII. *The Times*, London. 1918.

Records of the Great War, Vol VI. Chas. F. Horne. National Alumni, 1923.

Roger Keyes, Biography of. Cecil Aspinall-Oglander. Hogarth Press, London. 1951.

Royal Marine Commando. James D. Ladd. Hamlyn Publishing, London. 1985.

Supreme Courage. General Sir Peter de la Billiere. Time Warner Book Group, UK. 2004.

War Illustrated, The. Vol 8 – 9. The Amalgamated Press, London. 1918.

Zeebrugge and Ostend Dispatches etc. C. Sandford Terry. Oxford University Press, London. 1919.

Zeebrugge Museum. Pictorial souvenir. c 1920s.

Zeebrugge, Story of. Colonel Stinglhamber DSO. Zeebrugge Museum. 1928.

Memoirs of W. Wainwright. Everyman at War. Edited by C.B. Purdom. 1930.

Memoirs of Sergeant Harry Wright. Royal Marines Historical Society Special Publication. Number 12.

Birkenhead Advertiser, *Birkenhead News*, *Liverpool Daily Post*, *Liverpool Echo*, *Liverpool Evening Express*, *The Times*, *Wallasey News*. National Archives Kew.

The Yser and the Belgian Coast. Michelin Guide (Reprint) G.H. Smith, Easingwold, York, 1994.

ADM 116/1655 Operations off the Belgian Coast. Attack on Zeebrugge: Casualties.

ADM 1/8525/142 Naval Raids on Zeebrugge and Ostend.

FURTHER READING

In the aftermath of the raids on the Belgian ports, the public clamoured for a definitive account of the raids other than the released official statements. During his extensive tours of Britain and America, lecturing on the Zeebrugge raid, Captain Alfred F. B. Carpenter VC recognised the need for a definitive account of the raid. In August 1921, he published his outstanding account 'The Blocking of Zeebrugge'; such was the interest in the raid my 1926 edition was the seventh edition! This work forms the building block for probably every consecutive account of the raid. Due to the amount published, the title is freely available. Any contemporary publication, especially magazines, will inevitably cover the raids.

If this guide has stirred an interest in the raids, a visit to the Imperial War Museum or the National Archives at Kew will enhance your knowledge. As most of us are daunted by such a trip, your local library should be able to provide copies of the following freely available relatively modern recommended books.

A. F. B. Carpenter. *Blocking of Zeebrugge*. Reprinted Naval & Military Press, East Sussex 2006.

Deborah Lake. *The Zeebrugge & Ostend Raids 1918*. Pen & Sword, Barnsley 2002. A well written account but highly critical of Keyes.

Barrie Pitt. *Zeebrugge, 11 VCs before Breakfast*. Published Cassell Military Paperbacks, London. 1958 & 2003.

Philip Warner. *The Zeebrugge Raid*. William Kimber, London. 1978.

HMS *Vindictive* raised 16 August 1920.

Index

A selective index omitting continually occurring names and places.

British Individuals

Adams, Lieutenant Commander 69, 73
Aldridge, Private 94, 95, 104, 105
Alleyane, Lieutenant 115, 118, 119

Bacon, Admiral 30-37
Bamford, Captain VC 76, 81, 97, 129
Bayley, Admiral 25
Beatty, Admiral 27, 30, 36
Billyard-Leake Lieutenant 82, 86, 87, 104
Bonham Carter, Lieutenant 43, 84, 85
Bourke, Lieutenant VC 108, 121, 136
Bradford, Lieutenant Commander VC 70, 130, 141
Brock, Wing Commander 37, 44-46, 73
Brooks, Acting Captain 66

Campbell, Lieutenant 68,
Carden, Rear Admiral 30
Carpenter, Captain VC 53, 67, 68, 92, 99, 131
Chater, Captain 66, 69, 76, 97, 99, 102, 104
Chichester, Lieutenant Colonel 50
Churchill, Winston 7, 16, 25, 30, 37
Cooke, Lieutenant 76, 77, 99
Cordner, Major 65
Crutchley, Lieutenant VC 118, 120-122, 136, 137

Dawburn Young, Lieutenant 61, 82
Dean, Lieutenant VC 85, 88, 131
De Roebeck, Admiral 30

Dickinson, Lieutenant Commander 54
Drummond, Lieutenant VC 120, 121, 138

Elliot, Major 50, 53, 65, 66

Finch Sergeant VC 47, 71, 132
Forrester, Private 77, 78, 139
Franks, Lieutenant 43
Fryatt, Captain 23, 24, 149

Gaslee, General 29
Geddes, Sir 27, 37
Gibbs, Lieutenant Commander 71, 92, 93, 95
Godsal, Commander 43, 107, 115, 116, 118, 162
Grant, Captain 43, 44
Grayken Private 55

Halahan, Captain 53, 66
Hardy, Lieutenant Commander 107, 108, 115, 116
Harrison, Commander VC 73-75, 133
Hawkins, Lieutenant 70
Hilton Young, Lieutenant Commander 71, 93, 100
Holdridge, Private 45

Jellicoe, Admiral 25, 30, 35-37

Keyes, Geoffrey VC 31, 38

Lamplough, Lieutenant 77, 99
Lankshear Private 52
Lynes, Commodore 62, 116, 117, 122

McKenzie, Able Seaman VC 75, 134

174

Royal Air Force

British Units

Merchant Vessels

German Individuals

The Kaisers' Warships

German Batteries

Cemeteries

Memorlals.